Academic
Learning
Series

TCP/IP for
Microsoft®
Windows NT®

Lab Manual

Microsoft®*Press*

PUBLISHED BY
Microsoft Press
A Division of Microsoft Corporation
One Microsoft Way
Redmond, Washington 98052-6399

Copyright © 1998 by Microsoft Corporation

Library of Congress Cataloging-in-Publication Data
TCP/IP for Microsoft Windows NT / Microsoft Corporation.
    p.   cm.
  Includes index.
  ISBN 1-57231-623-3
  ISBN 0-7356-0522-X (Academic Learning Series)
  1. Electronic data processing personnel--Certification.
2. Microsoft software--Study and teaching. 3. TCP/IP (Computer
network protocol)   I. Microsoft Corporation.
QA76.3.M53 1997
004.6'2--dc21   97-20760
                                                                          CIP

Printed and bound in the United States of America.

2 3 4 5 6 7 8 9   WCWC   3 2 1 0 9

Distributed in Canada by ITP Nelson, a division of Thomson Canada Limited.

A CIP catalogue record for this book is available from the British Library.

Microsoft Press books are available through booksellers and distributors worldwide. For further information about international editions, contact your local Microsoft Corporation office or contact Microsoft Press International directly at fax (425) 936-7329. Visit our Web site at mspress.microsoft.com.

BackOffice, Microsoft, Microsoft Press, MS, MS-DOS, MSN, NetShow, Win32, Windows, the Windows logo, and Windows NT are either registered trademarks or trademarks of Microsoft Corporation in the United States and/or other countries. Other product and company names mentioned herein may be the trademarks of their respective owners.

Acquisitions Editor: William Setten
Series Editor: Barbara Moreland

Part No. 097-0002096

Introduction to Laboratory Exercises

Included with the Academic Learning Series (ALS) texts are hands-on lab exercises designed to give you practical experience using Microsoft Windows NT 4.0. This hands-on experience is an essential part of your training because it is difficult to truly understand and use the operating system and its features without having had the opportunity to explore firsthand the menus, options, and responses. The tasks included in these exercises provide an opportunity for you to test the concepts presented in the text and to use the utilities and tools of TCP/IP for Microsoft Windows NT.

The lab exercises are best used in a classroom setting, though some exercises can be completed individually. The exercises presume a classroom network setup in one or more Windows NT domains with shared resources (depending upon the specific ALS text being used).

The directory of subdirectories, programs, and data files designed to support these labs can be shared from the instructor's system or installed on each student's system. A lab setup guide is provided for the instructor to use in setting up the classroom to support the labs.

The lab exercises do not precisely mirror the text's practice activities. Domain names, user names, IP addresses, shared resources, and other specific references in the lab exercises may be somewhat different from similar references in the ALS text or from those used in setting up the classroom network.

Local constraints must be followed to ensure proper network operations. Since it is not possible to predict each institution's local networking requirements, your instructor will explain differences that occur.

The old saying "The way to get to Carnegie Hall is to practice, practice, practice" is equally true of the pursuit of personal competency and Microsoft Certification. The tests required for Microsoft Certified Product Specialist, Systems Engineer, or other Microsoft certifications are demanding. One of the best ways to become confident in the use of TCP/IP for Microsoft Windows NT is to complete each of the assigned lab exercises as well as the practice tasks included in the text.

Lab 1: Installing, Configuring, and Testing TCP/IP

Objectives

After completing this lab, you will be able to:

- Install TCP/IP.
- Manually configure TCP/IP parameters.
- Use the IPCONFIG utility to view configured IP parameters.
- Use the PING utility to test TCP/IP communications.
- Install Network Monitor.

Before You Begin

To complete this lab, you need a computer with Microsoft Windows NT Workstation or Microsoft Windows NT Server installed.

You will also need the following information. Refer to the next page for the configuration of the classroom.

When this information is required	Use
Subnet ID	255.255.255.0
Host ID	131.107.4.10
Gateway	131.107.4.1

Estimated time to complete this lab: 15 minutes

Classroom Configuration

The classroom configuration is set up as three physical segments, or subnets, connected by an IP router. The following illustration shows the classroom configuration.

Students are divided between two subnets. Students on subnet 1 (131.107.3.0) are assigned a unique student number that ends with an odd number. Students on subnet 2 (131.107.4.0) are assigned a unique student number that ends with an even number.

The instructor's server is on network 3 (131.107.2.0). This configuration was designed so that the instructions for accessing the instructor server are the same for each student network.

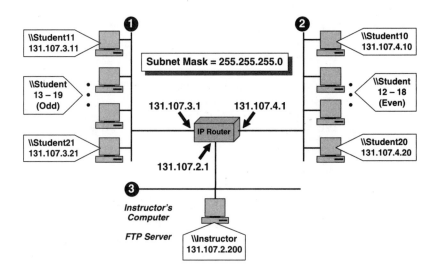

10

Exercise 1
Installing and Configuring TCP/IP

In this exercise, you will install and configure Microsoft TCP/IP. First you will remove the NWLink IPX/SPX transport from your workstation configuration.

➤ **To install TCP/IP**

1. Log on as Administrator with no password.

2. On the **Start** menu, point to **Settings** and then click **Control Panel**.

   The **Control Panel** appears.

3. Double-click **Network**.

   The **Network** dialog box appears.

4. Document the network services and protocols installed on your workstation. You will reference them later in the exercise.

Computer Browser	*NWLink*
MS IIS 2.0	*NWLink NetBios*
NetBios Interface	
RPC Configuration	
Server	
Workstation	

5. On the **Protocols** tab, select **NWLink IPX/SPX Compatible Transport Protocol**, and then click **Remove**.

   A warning box confirms the operation.

6. Click **Yes**.

   The **NWLink IPX/SPX Compatible Transport** no longer appears.

7. Click **Add**.

   The **Select Network Protocol** dialog box appears.

8. In the **Select Network Protocol** box, select **TCP/IP Protocol** and then click **OK**.

   The **TCP/IP Setup** dialog box appears, prompting you to install DHCP.

9. Click **No**.

   The **Windows NT Setup** box appears, prompting for the full path of the Windows NT distribution files.

10. Type **C:\I386** and then click **Continue**.

    The appropriate files are copied to your workstation.

➤   **To configure TCP/IP**

1. In the **Network** dialog box, click **Close**.

    Windows NT will display binding information and then the **Microsoft TCP/IP Properties** dialog box appears.

2. Type the following configuration information (refer to the "Before You Begin" section of this lab for your subnet ID and host ID):

In this box	Type
IP Address	**131.107.**_subnet_id.host_id_
Subnet Mask	**255.255.255.0**
Default Gateway	**131.107.**_subnet_id_**.1**

3. Click **OK**.

    A **Network Settings Change** dialog box appears indicating the computer needs to be restarted to initialize the new configuration.

4. Click **No**.

Important Do not shut down your computer. If you shut down and restart your computer, the following exercise will not work.

Exercise 2
Testing the TCP/IP Configuration

In this exercise, you will use the IPCONFIG utility to view an IP configuration and the PING utility to test your workstation configuration and connections to other TCP/IP hosts. You will see PING fail and succeed.

➤ **To test the configuration without initializing TCP/IP**

In this procedure, use the IPCONFIG utility to view the TCP/IP configuration when TCP/IP has not been initialized.

1. At a command prompt, type **ipconfig** and then press ENTER.

    Notice that the response is an empty table.

2. Ping the loopback address. Type:

    ping 127.0.0.1

    and then press ENTER.

3. Document the error message.

    Unable to contact IP driver, error code 2

4. Shut down and restart your computer.

➤ **To test the configuration with TCP/IP initialized**

1. Log on to the computer as Administrator, and open a command prompt.

2. Use the IPCONFIG utility to view the TCP/IP configuration.

3. Document the information that is supplied by the IPCONFIG utility.

    IP address 131.107.4.10
    Subnet Mask.... 255.255.255.0
    Gateway 131.107.4.1

4. Ping the loopback IP address to verify that the bindings for TCP/IP are correct. Type:

    ping 127.0.0.1

    and then press ENTER.

5. Could you ping successfully?

    Yes.

6. Ping the IP address of your workstation to verify that it was configured correctly. Type the following command, where y and z are your assigned subnet and host IDs:

    ping 131.107.y.z

    and then press ENTER.

7. Could you ping successfully?

    No.   Yes.

8. Ping the IP address of your default gateway to verify the configuration and connection. Type the following command, where y is your assigned subnet ID number:

    ping 131.107.y.1

    and press ENTER.

9. Could you ping successfully?

    No.   Yes.

10. Try to ping the IP address of another student. Type the following command, where y and z are the subnet and host IDs assigned to the other student:

    ping 131.107.y.z

    and press ENTER.

11. Ping an IP address that is not in use to see the error message. Type:

    ping 131.107.200.200

    and press ENTER.

12. Document the error message.

    Reply for 131.107.4.1: Dest. unreachable

Exercise 3
Installing Network Monitor

➤ **To install the Network Monitor**

1. Start **Control Panel**, double-click **Network**, and then click the **Services** tab.

2. Click **Add**.

   The **Select Network Service** dialog box appears.

3. In the **Network Service** list, click **Network Monitor Tools and Agent**, and then click **OK**.

   Windows NT Setup displays a dialog box asking for the full path to the Windows NT distribution files.

4. Type the path **C:\I386** and then click **Continue**.

   All necessary files, including the sample files, are copied to your hard disk.

5. In the **Network** dialog box, click **Close**.

6. When prompted, click **Yes** to restart your computer.

7. Log on as Administrator.

Note You will use Network Monitor to view packets in Lab 3.

Lab 2: Viewing and Modifying the ARP Cache

Objectives

After completing this lab, you will be able to:

- View the ARP cache.
- Modify an entry in the ARP cache.
- Modify the default gateway address.
- Test communication problems with incorrect parameters.

Estimated time to complete this lab: 15 minutes

Exercise 1
Viewing the ARP Cache

In this exercise, you will use the ARP utility to view entries in your computer's ARP cache.

➤ **To view the ARP cache**

1. At a command prompt, type **arp -g** and then press ENTER to view the ARP cache.

2. Document any entries.

Interface : 191.107.4.10 on Interface 2
Internet addr   Physical addr   type
191.107.4.1   00-c0-f0-0a-19-61   dynamic
191.107.4.16   00-c0-df-29-17-30   ,,

➤ **To ping a local host**

1. Ping the IP address of a student on your local network.

   This will add an entry to the cache.

2. View the new entry in the ARP cache.

3. What entry was added?

   191.107.4.12   dynamic

4. What is the entry's type?

   dynamic

➤ **To ping a remote host**

1. Ping the IP address of a host on a remote network (the instructor's server, 131.107.2.200).

2. View the entries in the ARP cache.

3. What entry was added to the ARP cache?

   191.107.4.12

4. Why was this entry added?

   local network

Exercise 2
Modifying the ARP Cache

In this exercise, you will use the ARP utility to modify entries in your computer's ARP cache.

➤ **To add an ARP entry**

1. View the ARP cache, and document the entry for your default gateway—for example: 131.107.*x*.1 08-00-02-6c-28-93.

   131. 107. 4. 1 00. c0. f0. 0a. f7-61

2. Type the following **arp** command to add the entry from step 1 to the cache. Type: **arp -s 131.107.***subnet_id***.1** *hardware_address*

   Note Make sure that you type the physical address using hyphens between as listed in step 1.

3. View the ARP cache to verify that the entry has been added.

4. What is the entry's type?

   Static

5. Why was this entry's type different from previous entries?

   me define it

6. To verify that the ARP cache entry for the default gateway is correct, ping a remote host.

Exercise 3
Identifying IP Address Resolution Problems

In this exercise, you will add an invalid hardware address for the default gateway to the ARP cache, and then configure the default gateway with an invalid IP address to see what happens when ARP cannot resolve an IP address to a hardware address.

➤ **To add an incorrect ARP entry**

In this procedure, you will add an entry into the ARP cache with an invalid hardware address, and then document the problem it causes in remote communications.

1. Use the **arp** command to change the hardware address of the default gateway. Type:

   arp -s 131.107._subnet_id_**.1 08-00-02-12-34-56**

2. Try to communicate with a remote host (the instructor's computer, **131.107.2.200**).

3. Were you successful? If not, document the error below.

   Yes, No! Request timed out

➤ **To remove the incorrect ARP entry**

1. Use the **arp** command to delete the incorrect entry from cache. Type:

   arp -d 131.107._subnet_id_.1

2. Try to communicate with a remote host (the instructor computer, **131.107.2.200**).

3. Were you successful? If not, document the error message below.

   Yes.

➤ **To configure the default gateway address incorrectly**

1. In the **Network** dialog box, click the **Protocols** tab.

2. Click **Properties**.

   The **Microsoft TCP/IP Properties** dialog box appears.

3. In the **Default Gateway** box, change the last octet to **199**.

4. Click **OK**.

   The **Network** dialog box appears.

5. Click **OK**.

➤   **To test the incorrect default gateway address**

1. Ping the IP address of your default gateway (**131.107.**subnet_id**.1**, not the incorrect address configured in the previous step).

2. Could you ping successfully? Why or why not?

    Yes, B/c the change hasn't been affecting yet

3. Ping a host on a remote network.

4. Could you ping successfully? Why or why not?

    _No._

5. Why could you ping the default gateway, but not a remote host?

➤   **To correct and test the correct default gateway address**

1. Restore the IP address of the default gateway to its original value.

2. To verify that the configuration of the default gateway is correct, ping the instructor's computer.

Lab 3: Viewing ICMP and ARP Packets

Objectives

After completing this lab, you will be able to:

- Capture and analyze ICMP packets with Network Monitor.
- Capture and analyze ARP packets with Network Monitor.

Estimated time to complete this lab: 20 minutes

Exercise 1
Examine an ICMP packet

In this exercise, you will use Network Monitor to capture and display packets.

➤ **To start Network Monitor**

1. On the **Start** menu, point to **Programs**, **Administrative Tools**, and then click **Network Monitor**.

   The **Network Monitor** window appears.

2. Maximize the **Network Monitor** window.

3. Maximize the **Capture** window.

➤ **To capture network data**

■ On the **Capture** menu, click **Start**.

   This starts the data capture process. Network Monitor allocates buffer space for network data and begins capturing frames.

➤ **To generate network traffic**

■ On your computer open a command prompt, and type:

   ping 131.107.2.200

➤ **To stop the network data capture**

1. Switch back to **Network Monitor**.

2. On the **Capture** menu in **Network Monitor**, click **Stop**.

   Network Monitor stops capturing frames and displays four panes: **Graph**, **Total Stats**, **Session Stats**, and **Station Stats**.

➤ **To view captured data**

■ On the **Capture** menu, click **Display Captured Data**.

   The **Network Monitor Capture Summary** window appears, displaying the summary record of all frames captured.

➤ **To highlight captured data**

In the following procedure, you will change the color of all frames that use ICMP. This is useful when viewing frames for a particular protocol.

1. On the **Display** menu, click **Colors**.

   The **Protocol Colors** dialog box appears.

2. Under **Name**, select **ICMP (Internet Control Message Protocol)**.

3. Under **Colors**, set **Foreground** to **Red**, and then click **OK**.

   The **Network Monitor Capture Summary** window appears, displaying all ICMP frames in red.

➤ **To view frame details**

1. Under **Description**, double-click an **ICMP** frame that has an entry of **Echo** in the description column.

   This frame shows an ICMP echo request from the client. Three separate windows are displayed. The top window displays the frame summary, the middle window displays the selected frame details, and the bottom window displays the selected frame details in hexadecimal notation.

2. In the **Detail** window, click **ICMP** with a plus sign (**+**) preceding it.

   The plus sign indicates that the information can be expanded by clicking it.

3. Expand the **ICMP** details.

   The **ICMP** properties expand to show more detail. The contents of the ICMP packet are highlighted and displayed in hexadecimal notation in the bottom window.

4. In the **Detail** window, click **ICMP: Packet Type = Echo**.

   What hexadecimal number corresponds with **ICMP: Packet Type = Echo**? (Record your data in the table that follows.)   *08*

5. In the **Detail** window, right-click **ICMP: Packet Type = Echo** and then click **Find Next Instance**.

   The **Find Frame Expression** dialog box appears, displaying information about the packet type.

6. Click **Cancel**.

7. In the **Detail** window, click **Checksum**.

   What is the **Checksum** number? (Record your data in the table below.) *0x E75B*

8. In the **Detail** window, click **Identifier**.

   What is the **Identifier** number? (Record your data in the table below.) *256 (0x100)*

9. In the **Detail** window, click **Sequence Number**.

   What is the **Sequence Number**? (Record your data in the table below.) *25856 (0x6500)*

10. In the **Detail** window, click **Data**.

    The data received in the echo message must be returned in the echo reply message.

11. Repeat steps 1 through 9 for the **Echo Reply** packet that follows the echo packet that is currently displayed.

    Which items have changed?

Field	Echo	Echo Reply
Packet Type	✓	✓
Checksum	✓	*0x EF5B*
Identifier		*256 (0x100)*
Sequence Number		*25856 (0x6500)*

➤ **To save the capture for later analysis**

1. On the **File** menu, click **Save As**.

2. Under **File Name**, type **ping.cap** and then click **OK**.

3. On the **File** menu, click **Close**.

   The **Network Monitor Capture** window appears, still displaying the statistics from the last capture.

4. Exit **Network Monitor**.

Exercise 2
Examine an ARP packet

In this exercise, you will use Network Monitor to capture and display ARP packets.

➤ **To capture network data**

1. Start Network Monitor.
2. On the **Capture** menu, click **Start**.
3. Open a command prompt, and type:

   ping 131.107.2.200
4. On the **Capture** menu in **Network Monitor**, click **Stop and View**.

   The **Network Monitor Capture Summary** window appears, displaying the summary record of all frames captured.
5. Maximize the **Capture** window.

➤ **To highlight captured data**

In the following procedure, you will change the color of all frames that use ARP.

1. On the **Display** menu, click **Colors**.

   The **Protocol Colors** dialog box appears.
2. Under **Name**, select **ARP_RARP**.
3. Under **Colors**, set **Foreground** to **Red**, and then click **OK**.

   The **Network Monitor Capture Summary** window appears, displaying all ARP frames in red.

➤ **To view the ARP request frame details**

1. Under **Description**, double-click the **ARP: Request**.
2. In the **Detail** window, click **Frame** with a plus sign (**+**) preceding it.
3. Expand the **Frame** details.

   What is the size of the base frame?

   42 bytes
4. Collapse the base frame properties.
5. In the **Detail** window, expand **ETHERNET**.

   The **ETHERNET** frame properties are displayed.

   What is the destination address?

   FFFFFFFFFFFF

6. Does the destination address refer to a physical address?

Yes   NO.

7. If the destination address does not refer to a physical address, what does it represent?

Hardw broadcast address.

8. What is the source address?

00 C 0D F E 7 A 6 17

9. What type of Ethernet frame is this?

ARP (0x 0806)

10. How many bytes did it take to identify this frame?

14 Bytes

11. How many bytes are remaining in the frame?

28 Bytes

12. What were the first 14 bytes used for?

13. Collapse the **ETHERNET** properties.

14. In the **Detail** window, expand **ARP_RARP**.

    What is the sender's hardware address?

00 C 0D F E 7 A 6 17

15. What is the sender's protocol address?

131. 107. 4. 10

16. What is the target's hardware address?

0 0000 0000 0000

17. What is the target's protocol address?

131. 107. 4. 1

18. Why is the target's hardware address all zeroes?

B/C not A/V

➤ **To examine an ARP reply**

1. Under **Description**, click **ARP: Reply**.

2. In the **Detail** window, expand **ETHERNET: ETYPE**.

   The **ETHERNET: ETYPE** frame properties are displayed.

3. What is the destination address?

   00 C0DFE7A617

4. Does the destination address refer to a physical address?

   Yes

5. What is the source address?

   _00C0F 00AF7B1_

6. What type of Ethernet frame is this?

   0x0806 (ARP)

7. How many bytes did it take to identify this frame?

   _14_

8. How many bytes are remaining in the frame?

   _46_

9. What were the first 14 bytes used for?

   ARP

10. Collapse the **ETHERNET** properties.

11. In the **Detail** window, expand **ARP_RARP**.

    What is the sender's hardware address?

    _00C0F 00AF7B1_

12. What is the sender's protocol address?

    _191.107.9.10_

13. What is the target's hardware address?

    00C0DFE7A617

14. What is the target's protocol address?

    _191.107.4.10_

15. Why is the target's hardware address no longer all zeroes?

16. Why did the router reply to the ARP request instead of the host that was pinged (131.107.2.200)?

Lab 4: Assigning IP Addresses

Objectives

After completing this lab, you will be able to:

- Determine valid address classes.
- Determine valid IP addresses.
- Identify network components requiring IP addresses.
- Assign IP addresses to hosts.
- Identify common IP addressing problems.

Estimated time to complete this lab: 35 minutes

Exercise 1
Determining the Address Class

In this exercise, you will determine the correct address class for a given IP address and scenario.

1. Write the address class next to each IP address.

Address	Class
131.107.2.89	B
3.3.57.0	A
200.200.5.2	~~B~~ C
191.107.2.10	B
127.0.0.1	Loopback (reserve)

2. Which address class(es) will allow you to have more than 1,000 hosts per network?

   A x B

3. Which address class(es) will allow only 254 hosts per network?

   C

*to determine the Network type → look
at the first OCTET.*

Exercise 2
Identifying Invalid IP Addresses

In this exercise, you will identify which of the following IP addresses cannot be
assigned to a host and then explain why it is invalid.

- Review the following IP addresses. Circle the portion of the IP address that
  would be invalid if it were assigned to a host, and then explain why it is
  invalid.

  a. 131.107.256.80 _Class b type - 256 is invalid
      max is 255._

  b. 222.222.255.222 _C type
      → allows up to 229 networks only_

  c. 231.200.1.1 _D type (can't use on internet)
      valid_

  d. 126.1.0.0 _A type (0 can't be use for host ID)_

  e. 0.127.4.100 _Invalid net ID._

  f. 190.7.2.0 _B type_

  g. 127.1.1.1 _Invalid net ID._

  h. 198.121.254.255 _C type (Invalid)_

  i. 255.255.255.255 _E type (Broadcast)
      Invalid_

Exercise 3
What Requires an IP Address?

In this exercise, you will decide which of the following network components require IP addresses in a TCP/IP network environment. When a protocol is listed, assume it is the only protocol installed on the host.

■ Review the following network components. Circle the letter that corresponds to the network components that do not require an IP address.

a.   Microsoft Windows NT computer running TCP/IP

b.   LAN Manager workstation that connects to a Windows NT computer running TCP/IP

c.   Windows 95 computer that requires access to shared resources on a Windows NT computer running TCP/IP

d.   UNIX host that you want to connect to using TCP/IP utilities

e.   Network interface printer running TCP/IP

f.   Router for connecting to a remote IP network

g.   Ethernet port on local router

h.   Microsoft LAN Manager workstation that is attempting to connect to a LAN Manager server running NetBEUI

i.   Windows for Workgroups computer that requires access to shared resources on a LAN Manager server running NetBEUI

j.   Serial plotter on a Windows NT computer running TCP/IP

k.   Network printer shared off a LAN Manager server running NetBEUI

l.   Communications server providing terminal access to TCP/IP host computers

m.   Your default gateway

Exercise 4
Assigning IP Addresses in a Local Area Network (LAN) Environment

In this exercise, you will decide which class of address will support the following IP network. Next, you will assign a valid IP address to each type of host to easily distinguish it from other hosts (for example, UNIX, Windows NT servers, or Windows NT workstations). Please note that all computers are on the same subnet.

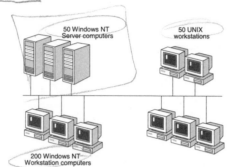

1. Which address classes will support this network?

   A / B   why? → # of users.

2. Which of the following network addresses will support this network?

   a. 197.200.3.0
   b. 11.0.0.0 ✓ A
   c. 221.100.2.0
   d. 131.107.0.0 ✓ B

3. Using the network ID that you chose, assign a range of host IDs to each type of host, so that you can easily distinguish the Windows NT Server computers from the Windows NT Workstation computers and from the UNIX workstations.

Type of TCP/IP host	IP address range
Windows NT Server computers	
UNIX workstations	
Windows NT Workstation computers	

Exercise 5
Determining the Required Number of IP Addresses

In this exercise, you will decide how many network IDs and host IDs are required to support this network.

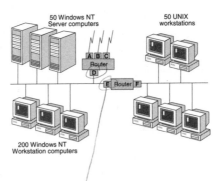

1. How many network IDs does this network environment require?

   50 A, B, C, E/D, F = 5

2. How many host IDs does this network environment require?

   50 306

3. Which default gateway (router interface) would you assign to the Windows NT Workstation computers that communicate primarily with the UNIX workstations?

   E

Exercise 6
Identifying IP Addressing Problems

In this exercise, you will review an example of an IP network, identify hidden IP addressing problems, and explain the possible effects caused by the problems.

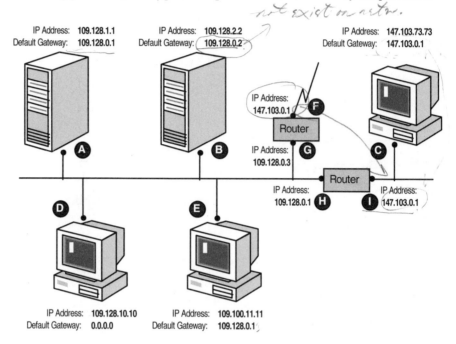

- List all IP addressing problems, and explain how each problem will affect communications.

_____

_____

_____

_____

_____

_____

Exercise 7
Determining the Effects of Duplicate IP Addresses

In this exercise, you will intentionally do something you should never do in real life—configure the local IP address to match the default gateway address. This will show you what happens when duplicate IP addresses exist on a network.

➤ **To configure a duplicate address**

1. Access the **Microsoft TCP/IP Properties** dialog box.

2. In the **IP Address** box, type the IP address of your default gateway.

3. Click **OK**.

   A **System Process – System Error** message box appears.

4. Click **OK**.

   The **Network** dialog box appears.

➤ **To view the error message caused by the duplicate address**

1. In the **Start** menu, point to **Programs**, **Administrative Tools**, and then click **Event Viewer**.

   The **Event Viewer** window appears.

2. Select the **System Log** error with a source of TCP/IP and view the details.

   The **Event Details** dialog box appears.

3. Document the contents of the error message.

   _____

   _____

   _____

   _____

4. Close **Event Viewer**.

➤ **To correct the duplicate address problem**

1. Open a command prompt.

2. View the TCP/IP configuration by typing **ipconfig** and then pressing ENTER.

   The IP Address has been changed dynamically and now is the same as the default gateway.

3. Exit the command prompt and switch to the **Network** dialog box.

4. Access the **Microsoft TCP/IP Properties** dialog box.

5. In the **IP Address** box, type your original IP address.

6. When you are finished, click **OK**.

   The **Network** dialog box appears.

7. Click **OK**.

8. Open a command prompt and use IPCONFIG to verify that your address is correctly configured.

Exercise 8
Identifying IP Addressing Problems

In this exercise, you will review an example of an IP network, identify hidden IP addressing problems, and explain the possible effects caused by the problems.

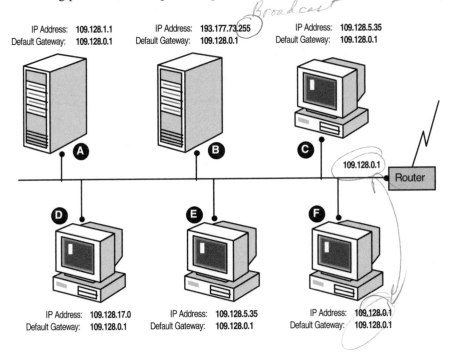

- List all IP addressing problems, and explain how each problem will affect communications.

Exercise 9 *(optional)*
Determining the Address Class

1. Which address class(es) will allow you to have 225 or more hosts per network?

   A, B, C

2. Which address class(es) will allow you to have 2000 hosts per network?

   A, B

Exercise 10 *(optional)*
Identifying Invalid IP Addresses

Classes A & B can have 255. [handwritten]

In this exercise, you will identify which of the following IP addresses cannot be assigned to a host and then explain why it is invalid.

- Review the following IP addresses. Circle the portion of the IP address that would be invalid if it were assigned to a host, and then explain why it is invalid.

  a. 181.7.255.80 ___OK___

  b. 122.222.255.222 ___A → OK___

  c. 193.0.255.1 ___C → its invalid OK___

  d. 127.1.0.0 ___NOT VALID___

  e. 10.127.4.100 ___OK___

  f. 190.7.2.0 ___OK___

Lab 5: Defining a Subnet Mask

Objectives

After completing this lab, you will be able to:

- Define subnet masks for class A, B, and C networks.
- Identify common problems associated with subnet masks.

Estimated time to complete this lab: 30 minutes

Exercise 1
Defining a Valid Subnet Mask

In this exercise, you will define a subnet mask for multiple situations. Not every situation requires subnetting.

1. Class A network address on a local network.

   255. 0. 0. 0

2. Class B network address on a local network with 4,000 hosts.

   _____

3. Class C network address on a local network with 254 hosts.

   255. 255

4. Class A address with 6 subnets.

   _____

5. Class B address with 126 subnets.

   _____

6. Class A network address. Currently, there are 30 subnets that will grow to approximately 65 subnets within the next year. Each subnet will never have more than 50,000 hosts.

   _____

7. Using the subnet mask from step 6, how much growth will this subnet mask provide?

   _____

8. Class B network address. Currently, there are 14 subnets that may double in size within the next two years. Each subnet will have fewer than 1,500 hosts.

   _____

9. Using the subnet mask from step 8, how much growth will this subnet mask provide?

   _____

Exercise 2
Determining the Effects of an Invalid Subnet Mask

In this exercise, you will configure your computer with an invalid subnet mask to see what happens when you try to communicate with a host on a local and remote network.

➤ **To modify the subnet mask**

1. Access the **Microsoft TCP/IP Properties** dialog box.

2. In the **Subnet Mask** box, type **255.255.255.248**, which is incorrect for the classroom network.

3. Click **OK**.

   The **Network** dialog box appears.

4. Click **OK**.

➤ **To test the new subnet mask**

1. Open a command prompt.

2. Use the IPCONFIG utility to view the configured parameters and verify that the change to the subnet mask has been implemented.

3. Ping the IP address of your default gateway, and then document the results.

   _____

   _____

4. Ping a host on your local network and document the results.

   _____

   _____

5. Convert your computer's IP address and the IP address of your default gateway to binary format, and then AND them to the subnet mask to determine why the subnet mask is invalid.

Your IP address	131.107.y.z	10000011 01101011
Subnet mask	255.255.255.248	11111111 11111111 11111111 11111000
Result		

Destination IP address (gateway)	131.107.y.z	10000011 01101011
Subnet mask	255.255.255.248	11111111 11111111 11111111 11111000
Result		

6. Did the result of ANDing indicate that the destination IP address and subnet mask were for a local or remote network?

_____

_____

7. What did you conclude about why you couldn't successfully ping your default gateway?

_____

_____

➤ **To test a different subnet mask**

1. Switch to the **Network** dialog box.

2. Change your subnet mask to **255.255.0.0** (this is also incorrect for the classroom network).

3. Switch to a command prompt and use IPCONFIG to verify the subnet mask change.

4. Ping a host on a remote network and document the results.

_____

_____

5. Ping a host on the local network and document the results.

_____

_____

6. Convert your IP address and the IP address of the remote host to binary format, and then AND them to the subnet mask to determine why the subnet mask is invalid.

Your IP address	131.107.y.z	1 0 0 0 0 0 1 1 0 1 1 0 1 0 1 1
Subnet mask	255.255.0.0	1 1 1 1 1 1 1 1 1 1 1 1 1 1 1 1 0 0 0 0 0 0 0 0 0 0 0 0 0 0 0
Result		

Destination IP address	131.107.y.z	1 0 0 0 0 0 1 1 0 1 1 0 1 0 1 1
Subnet mask	255.255.0.0	1 1 1 1 1 1 1 1 1 1 1 1 1 1 1 1 0 0 0 0 0 0 0 0 0 0 0 0 0 0 0
Result		

7. Did the result of ANDing indicate that the destination IP address and subnet mask were for a local or remote network?

_____

_____

8. What did you conclude about why you could not successfully ping a remote host?

_____

_____

➤ **To restore subnet mask to correct value**

1. Switch to the **Network** dialog box.

2. Restore your subnet mask to **255.255.255.0**.

3. Switch to a command prompt and use IPCONFIG to verify the subnet mask update.

4. Exit the command prompt.

5. Shut down and restart your computer.

6. Ping the IP address of your default gateway and a remote host to verify that the subnet mask is configured correctly.

7. Compare the error messages generated using incorrect subnet masks (earlier in this exercise) to see how differently TCP/IP responds when the subnet mask indicates a local versus remote network.

8. What did you conclude about how TCP/IP uses a subnet mask?

_____

_____

Exercise 3
Identifying Subnet Addressing Problems

In this exercise, you will review the following two examples, identify the hidden problems, and explain the possible effects caused by the problems.

Example 1

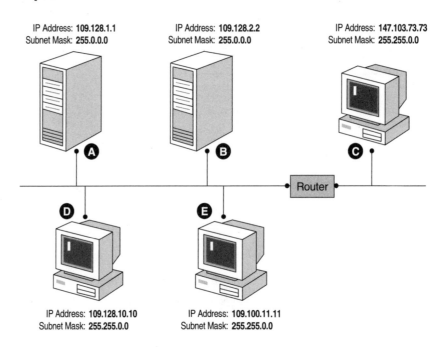

IP Address: **109.128.1.1**
Subnet Mask: **255.0.0.0**

IP Address: **109.128.2.2**
Subnet Mask: **255.0.0.0**

IP Address: **147.103.73.73**
Subnet Mask: **255.255.0.0**

Router

IP Address: **109.128.10.10**
Subnet Mask: **255.255.0.0**

IP Address: **109.100.11.11**
Subnet Mask: **255.255.0.0**

1. Which hosts have an incorrect subnet mask?

2. How will an invalid subnet mask affect these hosts?

3. What is the correct subnet mask?

Example 2

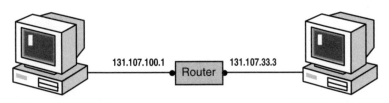

IP Address: **131.107.100.27**
Subnet Mask: **255.255.0.0**
Default Gateway: **131.107.100.1**

IP Address: **131.107.33.7**
Subnet Mask: **255.255.0.0**
Default Gateway: **131.107.33.3**

1. What is the problem with this subnet mask?

   _____

   _____

2. How will it affect communications?

   _____

   _____

3. What is the correct subnet mask?

   _____

   _____

Exercise 4
An Alternate Tutorial on Subnet Masking

Subnet masking is a topic that is central to your understanding of TCP/IP. The following is an alternate explanation, complete with examples, of subnet masking.

Remember that the Class of an IP address determines the maximum number of bits available for host addresses. Subnetting is the process of utilizing some of the bits normally available for the host address for additional networks or subnets within a company.

Class	Value of First Octet	Number of bits in the Network ID	Number of bits available for host address = n	Number of hosts available
A	1–127 with 127 reserved for diagnostics	8	24	$2^{24} - 2$
B	128–191	16	16	$2^{16} - 2$
C	192–223	24	8	$2^{8} - 2$

If we want to divide the host bits (represented by n) into subnets and hosts per subnet, we might say that we want x to represent the number of subnets, and y to represent the number of hosts per subnet. We would then have n host bits used to represent $2^{x} - 2$ subnets and $2^{y} - 2$ hosts per subnet, and x + y = n.

We subtract 2 in the above formulae because neither the value of the subnet nor the host address can be all 0s or all 1s.

If a company is assigned a Class B network number of 145.67.0.0, that company has 16 bits available for subnetting. If the company wants to support 65 subnets each with 200 hosts, then the value of $2^{x} - 2$ must be greater than or equal to 65 and the value of $2^{y} - 2$ must be greater than or equal to 200.

You may wish to refer to the following table for assistance:

X	$2^x - 2$
2	2
3	6
4	14
5	30
6	62
7	126
8	254
9	510
10	1022
11	2046
12	4094

Therefore, for the problem above, the value of x must be at least 5, and the value of y must be at least 7. Further, x+y must be 16. You could choose to use:

- 7 bits for subnetting and 9 bits for hosts per subnet, or
- 8 bits for subnetting and 8 bits for hosts per subnet, or
- 9 bits for subnetting and 7 bits for hosts per subnet.

We can represent the associated subnet masks as follow:

For 7 bits for subnetting and 9 bits for hosts per subnet, the subnet mask would be:

```
1 1 1 1 1 1 1 1 . 1 1 1 1 1 1 1 1 . 1 1 1 1 1 1 1 1 . 1 1 1 1 1 1 1 1
1 1 1 1 1 1 1 1 . 1 1 1 1 1 1 1 1 . 1 1 1 1 1 1 1 0 . 0 0 0 0 0 0 0 0
|___255____| |____255_____|. |___254___|. |_____0_____|
```

For 8 bits for subnetting and 8 bits for hosts per subnet, the subnet mask would be:

```
1 1 1 1 1 1 1 1 . 1 1 1 1 1 1 1 1 . 1 1 1 1 1 1 1 1 . 1 1 1 1 1 1 1 1
1 1 1 1 1 1 1 1 . 1 1 1 1 1 1 1 1 . 1 1 1 1 1 1 1 1 . 0 0 0 0 0 0 0 0
|___255____| |____255_____|. |___255___|. |_____0_____|
```

For 9 bits for subnetting and 7 bits for hosts per subnet, the subnet mask would be:

```
1 1 1 1 1 1 1 1 . 1 1 1 1 1 1 1 1 . 1 1 1 1 1 1 1 1 . 1 1 1 1 1 1 1 1
1 1 1 1 1 1 1 1 . 1 1 1 1 1 1 1 1 . 1 1 1 1 1 1 1 1 . 1 0 0 0 0 0 0 0
|___255____| |____255_____|. |___255___|. |___128_____|
```

1. Determine the appropriate values in the following table for the requirements given:

Network Number	Subnets needed	Number of hosts needed per subnet	Possible subnet mask
131.177.6.23	1000	1000	
194.67.89.0	4	4	
208.34.9.0	2	60	
150.56.0.0	500	1000	
125.0.0.0	1000	2000	

2. Which of the following IP address/subnet masks are illegal based on the fact that neither the subnet value nor the host portion of an IP address can be all 0s or all 1s?

   a. 142.56.78.128 with subnet mask of 255.255.255.240

   b. 131.107.3.3 with subnet mask of 255.255.255.0

   c. 198.0.0.7 with subnet mask of 255.255.255.240

Lab 6: Defining Network IDs for an Internetwork

Objective

After completing this lab, you will be able to:

■   Define a range of network IDs.

Before You Begin

Refer to the following illustration to complete the exercises.

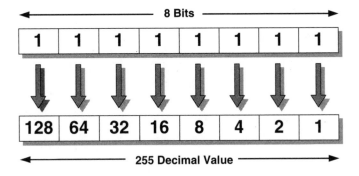

Estimated time to complete this lab: 30 minutes

Exercise 1
Defining a Range of Network IDs for Two Subnets

In this exercise, you will define a range of network IDs for an internetwork that consists of two subnets, using 2 bits from a class B subnet mask.

1. List all possible bit combinations for the following subnet mask, and then convert them to decimal format to determine the beginning value of each subnet.

255	255	192	0
1 1 1 1 1 1 1 1	1 1 1 1 1 1 1 1	**1 1 0 0 0 0 0 0**	0 0 0 0 0 0 0 0

Invalid   0 0 0 0 0 0 0 0   =   0

Subnet 1   _____   =   ____

Subnet 2   _____   =   ____

Invalid   1 1 0 0 0 0 0 0   =   192 (subnet mask)

2. List the range of host IDs for each subnet.

Subnet	Beginning value	Ending value
Subnet 1	*w.x.*____.1	*w.x.*____.254
Subnet 2	*w.x.*____.1	*w.x.*____.254

Exercise 2
Defining a Range of Network IDs for 14 Subnets

In this exercise, you will define a range of network IDs for an internet that consists of 14 subnets, using 4 bits from a class B subnet mask.

1. List all possible bit combinations for the following subnet mask, and then convert them to decimal format to determine the beginning value of each subnet.

255	255	240	0
1 1 1 1 1 1 1 1	1 1 1 1 1 1 1 1	**1 1 1 1** 0 0 0 0	0 0 0 0 0 0 0 0

Invalid   0 0 0 0 0 0 0 0   =   0

Subnet 1   _____   =   _____

Subnet 2   _____   =   _____

Subnet 3   _____   =   _____

Subnet 4   _____   =   _____

Subnet 5   _____   =   _____

Subnet 6   _____   =   _____

Subnet 7   _____   =   _____

Subnet 8   _____   =   _____

Subnet 9   _____   =   _____

Subnet 10   _____   =   _____

Subnet 11   _____   =   _____

Subnet 12   _____   =   _____

Subnet 13   _____   =   _____

Subnet 14   _____   =   _____

Invalid   1 1 1 1 0 0 0 0   =   240 (subnet mask)

2. List the range of host IDs for each subnet.

Subnet	Beginning value	Ending value
Subnet 1	*w.x.*_____.1	*w.x.*_____.254
Subnet 2	*w.x.*_____.1	*w.x.*_____.254
Subnet 3	*w.x.*_____.1	*w.x.*_____.254
Subnet 4	*w.x.*_____.1	*w.x.*_____.254
Subnet 5	*w.x.*_____.1	*w.x.*_____.254
Subnet 6	*w.x.*_____.1	*w.x.*_____.254
Subnet 7	*w.x.*_____.1	*w.x.*_____.254
Subnet 8	*w.x.*_____.1	*w.x.*_____.254
Subnet 9	*w.x.*_____.1	*w.x.*_____.254
Subnet 10	*w.x.*_____.1	*w.x.*_____.254
Subnet 11	*w.x.*_____.1	*w.x.*_____.254
Subnet 12	*w.x.*_____.1	*w.x.*_____.254
Subnet 13	*w.x.*_____.1	*w.x.*_____.254
Subnet 14	*w.x.*_____.1	*w.x.*_____.254

Exercise 3
Defining a Range of Network IDs Using a Shortcut

In this exercise, you will use a shortcut to define a range of network IDs for 14 subnets. Compare the results to the results in Exercise 2. The two should match. The first step has been done for you.

1. List the number of bits (in high order) that will be used for the subnet mask.

255	255	240	0
1 1 1 1 1 1 1 1	1 1 1 1 1 1 1 1	**1 1 1 1** 0 0 0 0	0 0 0 0 0 0 0 0

2. Convert the bit with the lowest value to decimal format.

_____

3. Convert the number of bits to decimal format (in low order), and then subtract 1 to determine the number of possible subnets.

_____

_____

4. Starting with 0, increment by the value calculated in step 2 the same number of times as the possible bit combinations calculated in step 3.

_____

_____

_____

_____

_____

_____

_____

_____

_____

_____

_____

_____

_____

_____

_____

Exercise 4 *(optional)*
Host IDs

Define a range of host IDs for each of the following subnets.

1. Network ID of 75.0.0.0, subnet mask of 255.255.0.0, and 2 subnets.

   _____

   _____

2. Network ID of 150.17.0.0, subnet mask of 255.255.255.0, and 4 subnets.

   _____

   _____

3. Network IDs of 107.16.0.0 and 107.32.0.0, subnet mask of 255.240.0.0, and 2 subnets.

   _____

   _____

4. Network IDs of 190.1.16.0, 190.1.32.0, 190.1.48.0, and 190.1.64.0, subnet mask of 255.255.248.0, and 4 subnets.

   _____

   _____

5. Network IDs of 154.233.32.0, 154.233.96.0, and 154.233.160.0, subnet mask of 255.255.224.0, and 3 subnets.

   _____

   _____

Exercise 5 *(optional)*
IP Addresses

In this exercise, you will determine the appropriate subnet mask for a given range of IP addresses.

1. Address range of 128.71.1.1 through 128.71.254.254.

    _____

    _____

2. Address range of 61,8.0.1 through 61.15.255.254.

    _____

    _____

3. Address range of 172.88.32.1 through 172.88.63.254.

    _____

    _____

4. Address range of 111.224.0.1 through 111.239.255.254.

    _____

    _____

5. Address range of 3.64.0.1 through 3.127.255.254.

    _____

    _____

Lab 7: Subnetting and Supernetting

Objectives

After completing this lab, you will be able to:

- Define a subnetting scheme for an internetwork.
- Define a supernetting scheme for an internetwork.

Estimated time to complete this lab: 30 minutes

Exercise 1
Defining a Subnet Addressing Scheme

In this exercise, you will work in a group to define a subnet addressing scheme based on one of the following scenarios.

For each scenario, you will define the following:

- A subnet mask.
- A range of valid network IDs.
- A default gateway for hosts on each subnet.

Scenario 1

You have been assigned one class B address of 131.107.0.0 by the InterNIC. Your private internet currently has five subnets. Each subnet has approximately 300 hosts. Within the next year the number of subnets will triple. The number of hosts on three of the subnets could increase to as many as 1,000.

1. How many bits did you use for the subnet mask?

2. How much growth did you allow for additional subnets?

3. How much growth did you allow for additional hosts?

Scenario 2

You have been assigned one class A address of 124.0.0.0 by the InterNIC. Your private internet currently has 5 subnets. Each subnet has approximately 500,000 hosts. In the near future, you'd like to divide the 5 subnets into 25 smaller, more manageable subnets. The number of hosts on the 25 new subnets could eventually increase to 300,000.

1. How many bits did you use for the subnet mask?

   _____

   _____

2. How much growth did you allow for additional subnets?

   _____

   _____

3. How much growth did you allow for additional hosts?

   _____

   _____

Scenario 3

You have 5 subnets with approximately 300 hosts on each subnet. Within the next 6 months, the number of subnets could increase to more than 100. The number of hosts on each subnet will probably never be more than 2,000. You don't have any plans to connect to the worldwide public Internet.

1. Which class of address did you use?

   _____

   _____

2. How many bits did you use for the subnet mask?

   _____

   _____

3. How much growth did you allow for additional subnets?

   _____

   _____

4. How much growth did you allow for additional hosts?

   _____

   _____

Scenario 4

An Internet service provider has just been assigned the block of 2,048 class C network numbers beginning with 192.24.0.0 and ending with 192.31.255.0.

1. What IP address would begin a "supernetted" route to this block of numbers?

   _____

2. What net mask would be used to supernet this block of numbers?

   _____

Customers of the Internet service provider have the following requirements:

- Customer 1 will not have more than 2,023 hosts.
- Customer 2 will not have more than 4,047 hosts.
- Customer 3 will not have more than 1,011 hosts.
- Customer 4 will not have more than 500 hosts.

Assign the missing IP and subnet mask values for each customer.

3. Customer 1

Beginning IP Address	192.24.0.1
Ending IP Address	192.24.7.8
Subnet Mask:	_____

4. Customer 2

Beginning IP Address	_____
Ending IP Address	192.24.31.254
Subnet Mask	255.255.240.0

5. Customer 3

Beginning IP Address	192.24.8.1
Ending IP Address	_____
Subnet Mask:	255.255.252.0

6. Customer 4

Beginning IP Address	192.24.14.1
Ending IP Address	192.24.15.254
Subnet Mask:	_____

Exercise 2 *(optional)*
Defining More Subnet Addressing Schemes

In this exercise, you will work in a group or by yourself to define a subnet addressing scheme based on one of the following scenarios.

For each scenario, you will define the following:

- A subnet mask.
- A range of valid network IDs.
- A default gateway for hosts on each subnet.

Scenario 1

You have been assigned one class A address of 101.0.0.0 by the InterNIC. Your private internet currently has five hundred subnets. Each subnet has approximately 300 hosts. Within the next year the number of subnets will triple. The number of hosts on three of the subnets could increase to as many as 2700.

1. How many bits did you use for the subnet mask?

   _____

   _____

2. How much growth did you allow for additional subnets?

   _____

   _____

3. How much growth did you allow for additional hosts?

   _____

   _____

Scenario 2

You have been assigned one class C address of 212.200.101.0 by the InterNIC. Your private internet currently has 5 subnets. Each subnet has approximately 10 hosts. In the near future, you'd like to divide the 5 subnets into 10 smaller, more manageable subnets. The number of hosts on the 10 new subnets could eventually increase to 20.

1. How many bits did you use for the subnet mask?

   _____

   _____

2. How much growth did you allow for additional subnets?

   _____

   _____

3. How much growth did you allow for additional hosts?

   _____

   _____

Lab 8: Viewing and Modifying the Routing Table

Objectives

After completing this lab, you will be able to:

- View a routing table.
- Add an entry to the routing table.
- Test communication problems with incorrect route entries.

Estimated time to complete this lab: 20 minutes

Exercise 1
Viewing the Routing Table

In this exercise, you will use the ROUTE utility to view entries in your local routing table.

➤ **To view the routing table**

1. Open a command prompt, type **route -p print**, and then press ENTER.

2. What address, other than your IP address and the loopback address, is listed under **Gateway Address**?

_____

_____

➤ **To remove the default gateway address**

In this procedure, you will remove the address for the default gateway. This will prevent any packets being sent to the default gateway for routing, and require all routing to be done from existing route entries.

1. Access the Microsoft TCP/IP Properties dialog box.

2. Delete the **Default Gateway** address.

3. Click **OK**.

4. Click **OK**.

➤ **To view the routing table**

1. Switch to the command prompt and use the **route print** command.

2. Is the default gateway address listed under **Gateway Address**?

_____

_____

➤ **To attempt network communication**

In this procedure, you will attempt communication with both local and remote hosts.

1. Ping the IP address of a student on the local network.

2. Was the ping successful?

_____

_____

3. Ping the IP address of the instructor's computer (131.107.2.200).

4. Was the ping successful? If not, what was the response?

_____

_____

➤ **To add a route entry**

In this procedure, you will add a static routing table entry for the router.

1. Type the following command where *x* is the IP address.

   route add 131.107.2.0 mask 255.255.255.0 131.107.*x*.1.

2. View the entries in the route table, and verify that the route is listed before you continue.

3. Ping the instructor computer (131.107.2.200).

4. Was the ping successful? If not, what was the response?

_____

_____

5. Ping a host on another student network.

6. Was the ping successful? Why or why not?

_____

_____

➤ **To restore the default gateway address**

In this procedure, you will restore the address for the default gateway. This will allow packets to be sent to the default gateway when no route entry exists for the destination network.

1. Access the Microsoft TCP/IP Properties dialog box.

2. In the **Default Gateway** box, type your default gateway address.

3. Click **OK**.

4. Click **OK**.

➤ **To test communication**

In this procedure, you will test the configured default gateway address to verify that internetwork operations are successful.

1. Switch to the command prompt and use the **route print** command to view the routing table.

2. Is the default gateway address listed under **Gateway Address**?

_____

_____

3. Ping hosts on each network to verify that communication can be established.

Lab 9: Implementing DHCP

Objectives

After completing this lab, you will be able to:

- Install the DHCP Server service.
- Configure a DHCP server.
- Test the DHCP configuration.
- Troubleshoot DHCP.

Before You Begin

In this lab, you will work with a partner. Each of your computers will take on separate roles: one computer will be a DHCP server and the other computer will be a DHCP client.

Estimated time to complete this lab: 60 minutes

Exercise 1
Installing and Configuring DHCP Server

In this exercise, you will install and configure a DHCP server to automatically assign TCP/IP configuration information to DHCP clients.

Note Complete this procedure from the DHCP server only. In the next exercise, you will work with a partner to configure the other computer as a DHCP client.

➤ **To determine the network adapter card address**

In this procedure, you will determine the physical hardware address of your network adapter card. This address will be used to create a client reservation.

1. Open a command prompt, type **ipconfig /all**, and then press ENTER.
2. Document the physical address here for reference, without the hyphens (**-**).

_____

3. There are at least two other ways to check the physical address of your network adapter card. What are they?

_____

_____

_____

➤ **To install the DHCP Server service**

Note Complete this procedure from the DHCP server only.

1. Click **Start**, point to **Settings**, and then click **Control Panel**.
2. Double-click **Network**.

   The **Network Settings** dialog box appears.
3. Click the **Services** tab.
4. Click **Add**.

   The **Select Network Service** dialog box appears.

5. Select **Microsoft DHCP Server**, and then click **OK**.

   The **Windows NT Setup** box appears, prompting for the full path of the Windows NT distribution files.

6. Type **C:\I386** and then click **Continue**.

   The appropriate files are copied to your computer, and then a message box appears, informing you that a static IP address is now required for the network adapter card.

7. Click **OK**.

   The **Network** dialog box appears.

8. Click **Close**.

   The **Network Settings Change** dialog box appears, indicating that the computer needs to be restarted to initialize the new configuration.

9. Click **Yes**.

10. Log on as Administrator.

➤ **To create a DHCP scope**

In this procedure, you will create a DHCP scope that consists of one IP address (your partner's) with an assigned lease time of 1 day.

Note Complete this procedure from the DHCP server only.

---

1. Click **Start**, point to **Settings**, and then click **Control Panel**.

2. Double-click **Services.** What are the names of the DHCP services?

   _____

   _____

3. Close the **Services** dialog box.

4. Click **Start**, point to **Programs**, **Administrative Tools**, and then click **DHCP Manager**.

   The **DHCP Manager** window appears.

5. Under **DHCP Servers**, double-click ***Local Machine***.

6. On the **Scope** menu, click **Create**.

   The **Create Scope** dialog box appears.

7. Configure the scope using the following information:

In this box	Type this
IP Address Pool Start Address	Your partner's IP address
IP Address Pool End Address	Your partner's IP address
Subnet Mask	**255.255.255.0**
Lease Duration Limited To (Days)	**1**

8. Click **OK**.

   A **DHCP Manager** message box appears, indicating that the scope was successfully created, and now needs to be activated.

9. To activate the scope, click **Yes**.

   The **DHCP Manager** window appears with the new scope added. Notice the yellow lightbulb next to the IP address, indicating an active scope. A message box informs you that no more data is available.

10. Click **OK**.

➤ **To configure DHCP scope options**

In this procedure, you will create a DHCP scope option that automatically assigns a default gateway address to DHCP clients.

Note Complete this procedure from the DHCP server only.

---

1. On the **DHCP Options** menu, select **Scope**.

   The **DHCP Options: Scope** dialog box appears.

2. Under **Unused Options**, select **003 Router**, and then click **Add**.

   The **003 Router** option moves to the **Active Options** box.

3. Click **Value**.

   The **DHCP Options: Scope** dialog box expands to add the **Router IP Address** values box.

4. Click **Edit Array**.

   The **IP Address Array Editor** dialog box appears.

5. Under **New IP Address**, type your default gateway address (**131.107.***subnet_id***.1**), and then click **Add**.

   The new IP address appears under **IP Addresses**.

6. Click **OK** to return to the **DHCP Options: Scope** dialog box.

   The new router is listed in the IP address list.

7. Click **OK**.

   A message box informs you that no more data is available.

8. Close **DHCP Manager**.

Note You must exit and restart DHCP Manager to view the new options in the left pane.

➤   **To add a client lease reservation**

In this procedure, you will create a reservation for your partner's computer. This will ensure that each DHCP server is able to lease an address to a unique DHCP client in an environment of multiple DHCP servers (as in the classroom environment).

Note   Complete this procedure from the DHCP server only.

1. Ping your partner's IP address, and then type **arp -a** to obtain the physical address of your partner's network adapter. Document the address here for reference. (Do **not** include hyphens in the physical address.)

2. Start **DHCP Manager**.
3. Double-click ***Local Machine***.

   The lightbulb icon and the IP address appear.
4. Click the lightbulb icon.

   The **Option Configuration** window displays an active scope option of 003 Router.
5. On the **Scope** menu, click **Add Reservations**.

   The **Add Reserved Clients** dialog box appears.
6. In the **IP Address** box, type your partner's IP address.
7. In the **Unique Identifier** box, type the physical address of your partner's network adapter.

Note   Do not include hyphens in the physical address.

8. In the **Client Name** box, type **student**x (where x is your partner's assigned number), and then click **Add**.

   The **Add Reserved Clients** dialog box appears.
9. To return to **DHCP Manager**, click **Close**.

Exercise 2
Testing the DHCP Configuration

In this exercise, you will test the DHCP server configuration by starting DHCP client on your partner's computer, and determining the TCP/IP configuration information assigned to it by the DHCP server.

Note This computer will become the DHCP client, and should have the physical address and computer name that was used to create the DHCP client reservation.

➤ **To install DHCP client**

1. From the Microsoft TCP/IP Properties dialog box, click the **IP Address** tab.

2. Click **Obtain an IP address from a DHCP server**.

   You will be prompted to enable DHCP.

3. Click **Yes**.

4. Click **OK**.

   This installs and activates the DHCP client on your computer.

5. Click **OK**.

➤ **To verify the DHCP-assigned TCP/IP information**

Note Complete this procedure from the DHCP client only.

1. At a command prompt, type **ipconfig /all** to view the TCP/IP configuration.

2. What IP address was assigned to the DHCP client computer by the DHCP server?

   _____

   _____

3. Verify that the DHCP server address is correct.

   _____

   _____

4. What is the address of the default gateway?

   _____

   _____

Exercise 3
Troubleshooting DHCP

In this exercise, you will troubleshoot various DHCP configuration errors.

Note This exercise contains procedures for both computers. Make sure you complete the correct procedure on the correct computer.

➤ **To view DHCP-assigned addresses**

In this procedure, you will view the DHCP server listing of leased addresses.

Note Complete this procedure from the DHCP server only.

1. In the **DHCP Manager** window, select the local scope (designated by the lightbulb icon).
2. From the **Scope** menu, click **Active Leases**.

   The **Active Leases** dialog box appears, displaying the list of IP addresses that have been leased to clients.
3. Click **Properties**.

   The **Client Properties** dialog box appears. The **Lease expires time** is listed as **infinite**.
4. To return to the **Active Leases** dialog box, click **OK**.
5. To return to the **DHCP Manager** window, click **OK**.

➤ **To renew a DHCP lease**

In this procedure, you will renew the lease assigned to the DHCP client computer.

Note Complete this procedure from the DHCP client only.

1. Open a command prompt and type **ipconfig /all**.
2. When does the lease expire?

   _____

   _____

3. To renew the lease, type **ipconfig /renew** at a command prompt and then press ENTER.

   The Windows IP Configuration information is displayed.
4. Type **ipconfig /all** to view the lease information.
5. When does the lease expire?

   _____

   _____

➤ **To stop the DHCP Server service**

In this procedure, you will stop the Microsoft DHCP Server service to prevent IP address lease assignments and renewals.

Note Complete this procedure from the DHCP server only.

1. Click **Start**, point to **Settings**, and then click **Control Panel**.
2. Double-click **Services**.
3. The **Services** dialog box appears.
4. Select **Microsoft DHCP Server** and then click **Stop**.

   A dialog box appears and prompts you to verify your selection.
5. Click **Yes**.

➤ **To attempt lease renewal**

In this procedure, you will use the IPCONFIG utility to attempt to renew the lease assigned to the DHCP client computer and determine the effects of the DHCP server being unavailable.

Note Complete this procedure from the DHCP client only.

---

1. Open a command prompt, type **ipconfig /renew**, and then press ENTER.
2. What message did you receive?

   _____

3. Use the PING utility to verify that TCP/IP can communicate with the instructor's server (131.107.2.200).

   PING should respond with four success messages.

   Even though you were unable to renew your IP address lease, it is still a valid lease (it has not expired), so TCP/IP communications are still possible.

➤ **To release a DHCP address**

In this procedure, you will use the IPCONFIG utility to release the IP address lease assigned to the DHCP client computer.

Note Complete this procedure from the DHCP client only.

---

1. Open a command prompt, type **ipconfig /release**, and then press ENTER.

   The Windows IP Configuration information appears.

2. What message did you receive?

   _____

3. Use the PING utility to test TCP/IP communications with the instructor's server (131.107.2.200).

   PING should respond with four "Destination host unreachable" messages.

4. Shut down and restart the DHCP client computer.

   Notice that it takes a long time for Windows NT Server to initialize. A **DHCP Client** message appears, indicating that the DHCP client was unable to obtain an IP network address from a DHCP server. You are asked if you want to see future DHCP messages.

5. Click **Yes**.

6. Open a command prompt and type **ipconfig /all** to view the IP configuration.

   The **Windows NT IP Configuration** dialog box appears. Notice that the IP address is set to **0.0.0.0**.

➤ **To start the DHCP Server service**

In this procedure, you will start the Microsoft DHCP Server service to allow IP address lease assignments and renewals.

Note Complete this procedure from the DHCP server only.

1. Click **Start**, point to **Settings**, and then click **Control Panel**.
2. Double-click **Services**.
3. The **Services** dialog box appears.
4. Select **Microsoft DHCP Server** and then click **Start**.

   A message box appears, verifying the start-up of DHCP Server.

➤ **To renew a DHCP lease**

In this procedure, you will use the IPCONFIG utility to renew the lease assigned to the DHCP client computer.

Note Complete this procedure from the DHCP client only.

1. Open a command prompt, type **ipconfig /renew**, and then press ENTER.
2. Type **ipconfig /all** and then press ENTER.
3. When does the lease expire?

   _____

   _____

4. To verify that the DHCP server can lease an IP address, restart the DHCP client computer.

Exercise 4
Resetting DHCP Services

In this exercise, you will reconfigure the DHCP Server computer and the DHCP client computer for future labs.

➤   **To stop the DHCP Server service**

Note   Complete this procedure from the DHCP server only.

---

1. Click **Start**, point to **Settings**, and click **Control Panel**.
2. Double-click **Services**.

   The **Services** dialog box appears.
3. Click **Microsoft DHCP Server** and then click **Stop**.
4. Click **Startup**.

   The **Service** dialog box appears.
5. Click **Manual** and then click **OK**.
6. Click **Close**.

➤   **To use a static IP address**

Note   Complete this procedure from the DHCP client only.

---

1. Click **Start**, point to **Settings**, and click **Control Panel**.
2. Double-click **Network**.

   The **Network** dialog box appears.
3. Click the **Protocols** tab and then click **Properties**.
4. Click **Specify an IP address**.
5. Type the following configuration information:

In this box	Type
IP Address	**131.107.**_subnet_id.host_id_
Subnet Mask	**255.255.255.0**
Default Gateway	**131.107.**_subnet_id_**.1**

6. Click OK.

   The **Network** dialog box appears.
7. Click OK.
8. Shut down and restart your computer.

Exercise 5 *(optional)*
Reversing Roles

In this exercise, you and your partner will switch roles and then repeat Exercises 2, 3, and 4.

➤ **To reverse roles**

1. Reconfigure the DHCP client computer as a Windows NT Server computer with the Microsoft DHCP Server service running.

2. Reconfigure the DHCP Server computer as a DHCP client computer.

3. Repeat Exercises 2, 3, and 4.

Lab 10: Installing, Configuring, and Monitoring DHCP Relay Agent

Objectives

After completing this lab, you will be able to:

- Install a DHCP relay agent.
- Configure a DHCP relay agent.
- Monitor DHCP packets.

Before You Begin

Address of the DHCP Server: **131.107.2.200**

Estimated time to complete this lab: 30 minutes

Exercise 1
Install and Configure DHCP Relay Agent

In this exercise, only one computer on each subnet will install DHCP Relay Agent. The instructor will designate the computer that DHCP Relay Agent will run on. This exercise must be completed on each subnet before starting Exercise 2.

Note Complete this exercise only on the computer that the instructor designates as the DHCP relay computer for your subnet.

➤ **To install DHCP Relay Agent**

1. Click **Start**, point to **Settings**, and click **Control Panel**.

2. Double-click **Network**.

   The **Network** dialog box will appear.

3. Click the **Services** tab.

   The **Services** tab will display the list of Network Services currently running on this computer.

4. Click **Add**.

   The **Select Network Service** dialog box displays the Network Services available.

5. Click **DHCP Relay Agent**.

   The DHCP Relay Agent is highlighted in the listbox.

6. Click **OK**.

   The **Windows NT Setup** dialog box appears.

7. Type the path to the Windows NT Server files and then click **Continue**.

   The **Network** dialog box appears.

8. Click **Close**.

   The **Unattended Setup** dialog box appears.

   You are prompted to add an IP address to the DHCP Servers list.

9. Click **Yes**.

   The **TCP/IP Properties** dialog box appears.

10. Click the **DHCP Relay** tab and then click **Add**.

    The **DHCP Relay Agent** property sheet appears.

11. Type the IP address of the DHCP Server (**131.107.2.200**) and click **Add**.

    The IP address **131.107.2.200** will be added to the **DHCP Servers** list.

12. Click **OK**.

    You will be prompted to reboot your computer.

13. Click **Yes**.

    Your computer will reboot with DHCP Relay Agent enabled.

Exercise 2
Start Network Monitor

In this exercise, you will start Network Monitor to capture DHCP packets.

Important The DHCP relay computers that were configured on each subnet in Exercise 1 must be running before beginning this exercise.

➤   **To start Network Monitor**

Note Complete this procedure from all computers except for the two designated DHCP relay computers.

1. Click Start, point to Programs, Administrative Tools, and then click Network Monitor.
2. Maximize the **Network Monitor** window.
3. Maximize the **Capture Window**.
4. On the **Capture** menu, click **Start Capture**.

Exercise 3
Install DHCP Client and view DHCP Packets

In this exercise, you will install DHCP client.

➤ **To install DHCP client**

Note Complete this procedure from all computers except for the two designated DHCP relay computers.

1. Access the Microsoft TCP/IP Properties dialog box.
2. Click **Obtain an IP address from a DHCP server**.

   A message box appears prompting you to enable DHCP.
3. Click **Yes**.
4. Click **OK**.
5. Click **OK**.
6. Open a command prompt and type:

   ipconfig /all

   Make sure that the lease date information is not blank. If your lease date information is blank, then repeat step 6 until it is resolved by DHCP.
7. Switch back to **Network Monitor**.
8. Click **Capture** and then click **Stop and View**.
9. You should have four DHCP packet types. What are these four types?

   _____

   _____

10. Which computer was the source for the Discover packet?

    _____

11. Which computer was the destination for the Discover packet?

    _____

12. What type of network was this packet transmitted on? (Hint: Check DHCP: Hardware type.)

    _____

13. What is the client Ethernet address?

    _____

14. Is the IP address of the router, DHCP relay agent, or DHCP Server known at this time?

    _____

15. What is the client Ethernet address?

_____

16. What is another way to check the Ethernet address on your computer?

_____

17. What is the offered IP address?

_____

18. What is the subnet mask?

_____

19. What is the length of the lease?

_____

20. What is the IP address of the offering DHCP Server?

_____

21. What is the IP address of the router?

_____

22. What is the IP address of the DHCP relay agent?

_____

Exercise 4
Disable DHCP Relay Agent

In this exercise, you will set the computers to their original configuration.

➤   **To disable the DHCP relay agent**

Note   Complete this procedure only from the DHCP relay computers.

---

1. Click **Start**, point to **Settings**, and click **Control Panel**.
2. Double-click **Services**.

   The **Services** dialog box will appear.
3. Click **DHCP Relay Agent**.
4. Click **Startup** tab.

   The **Service** dialog box appears.
5. Click **Disabled**.
6. Click **OK**.
7. Click **Close**.
8. Shutdown and restart your computer.

➤   **To use a static IP address**

Note   Complete this procedure only from the DHCP client computers.

---

1. Access the Microsoft TCP/IP Properties dialog box.
2. Click **Specify an IP address**.
3. Type the following configuration information.

In this box	Type
IP Address	**131.107.**subnet_id.host_id
Subnet Mask	**255.255.255.0**
Default Gateway	**131.107.**subnet_id.**1**

4. Click OK.

   The **Network** dialog box appears.
5. Click **OK**.
6. Shut down and restart your computer.

Lab 11: Resolving NetBIOS Names

Objectives

After completing this lab, you will be able to:

- Configure and use the LMHOSTS file.
- Troubleshoot NetBIOS name resolution.

Before You Begin

Note Wherever you see the term *%systemroot%*, substitute the name of the directory into which you installed Windows NT.

Estimated time to complete this lab: 35 minutes

Exercise 1
Configuring the LMHOSTS File

In this exercise, you will configure the LMHOSTS file to resolve NetBIOS names to IP addresses.

➤ **To attempt to resolve a remote computer name**

In this procedure, you will see what happens when you attempt to resolve a remote NetBIOS computer name (\\INSTRUCTOR) using just a local broadcast.

1. Start **Windows NT Explorer**.
2. On the **Tools** menu, click **Map Network Drive**.

   The **Map Network Drive** dialog box appears.
3. In the **Path** box, type **\\instructor** and then click **OK**.
4. What was the response?

   _____

   _____

5. Click **OK**.
6. Click **Cancel**.
7. Close **Windows NT Explorer**.

➤ **To configure LMHOSTS for remote computer names**

In this procedure, you will see what happens when you attempt to resolve a remote NetBIOS computer name with a properly configured LMHOSTS file.

1. Open a command prompt.
2. Using **edit**, change the applicable file, as follows:

Client type	Directory and file
Windows NT Server or Windows NT Workstation	*%systemroot%*\SYSTEM32\DRIVERS\ETC\LMHOSTS.SAM

3. At the beginning of the LMHOSTS file, read the instructions for adding entries.
4. Go to the end of the file, and add the following entry:

   131.107.2.200   instructor
5. Save the file as LMHOSTS.
6. Start **Windows NT Explorer**.
7. On the **Tools** menu, click **Map Network Drive**.

   The **Map Network Drive** dialog box appears.

8. In the **Path** box, type **\\instructor** and then click **OK**.

9. What was the response?

_____

_____

10. Edit the LMHOSTS file and add the NetBIOS name/IP address mappings of student computers located on a remote network (even-numbered students are on a separate network from odd-numbered students).

11. Save and exit the file.

12. Using **Windows NT Explorer**, verify that each entry is correct by viewing the shared resources of the computer.

    Success is indicated by a list of shared resources (or an empty list).

    If you receive an error message, compare the command syntax to the spelling of the LMHOSTS file entry.

Exercise 2
Identifying NetBIOS Name Resolution Problems

In this exercise, you will identify NetBIOS name resolution problems that occur when LMHOSTS file entries are invalid.

➤ **To copy the course lab files**

In this procedure, you will copy the course lab files from the **688** course compact disc.

1. Create the directory **C:\LabFiles** on your computer.

2. Insert the **688** course compact disc into the CD-ROM drive.

3. From Windows NT Explorer, copy the contents of the LabFiles directory on the **688** course compact disc to **C:\LabFiles**.

➤ **To prepare the computer**

In this procedure, you will copy an LMHOSTS file with invalid entries to your computer.

1. Rename the LMHOSTS file in the *%systemroot%*\SYSTEM32\drivers\etc directory to **LMHOSTS.OLD**.

2. Copy the LMHOSTS files (**LMHOSTS.***) from **C:\LabFiles\Lab11** to the *%systemroot%*\SYSTEM32\drivers\etc directory.

➤ **To use the NetBIOS name cache for resolution**

1. At a command prompt, verify that there is no session to \\INSTRUCTOR. Type:

   net use \\instructor\ipc$ /d

   This will remove any IPC$ session from earlier browsing attempts to \\INSTRUCTOR.

2. Purge the NetBIOS name cache. Type **nbtstat -R** and then press ENTER (the **-R** must be uppercase).

3. Try to browse \\INSTRUCTOR. Type **net view \\instructor** and then press ENTER.

4. Document the error that occurs when an entry for a remote host does not exist in the LMHOSTS file or when an entry is invalid.

   _____

   _____

5. To update the LMHOSTS file with an entry that includes the **#PRE** tag, copy LMHOSTS.PRE to LMHOSTS.

6. View the contents of the LMHOSTS file.

7. Document the entry.

_____

_____

8. View the NetBIOS name cache. Type **nbtstat -c** and then press ENTER.

   The entry does not appear in the name cache.

9. Use the NBTSTAT utility to load the **#PRE**-tagged entry into the NetBIOS name cache. Type **nbtstat -R** and then press ENTER (the -**R** must be uppercase).

10. View the NetBIOS name cache. Type **nbtstat -c** and then press ENTER.

11. Document the entries that appear.

_____

_____

12. View the instructor server shared resources. Type **net view \\instructor** and then press ENTER.

    A listing of shared resources appears.

13. Delete the LMHOSTS file.

14. Exit the command prompt.

Exercise 3
Identifying LMHOSTS File Entries

In this exercise, you will use the following illustration to determine which entries should be added to an LMHOSTS file for each network, so that hosts on network A can communicate with hosts on network B, and vice versa.

- Add the appropriate entries to the following LMHOSTS files so that hosts on both networks can communicate with each other.

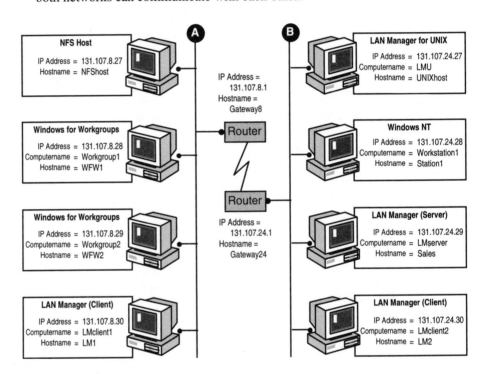

LMHOSTS File for Hosts on Network A

IP address	Name

LMHOSTS File for Hosts on Network B

IP address	Name

Lab 12: Implementing WINS

Objectives

After completing this lab, you will be able to:

- Use the WINS proxy agent to resolve remote NetBIOS names.
- Install a WINS server.
- Configure the DHCP server for WINS.
- Test the WINS configuration.

Before You Begin

In this lab, you will work with a partner. One computer on each subnet will be designated as a WINS proxy agent.

Note Wherever you see the term *%systemroot%*, substitute the name of the directory into which you installed Windows NT.

Estimated time to complete this lab: 45 minutes

Exercise 1
Installing a WINS Server

In this exercise, you will install a WINS Server to automatically resolve NetBIOS names to IP addresses for WINS clients.

Note Complete this exercise from the DHCP server computers.

➤ **To install the WINS Server service**

1. Click **Start**, point to **Settings**, and then click **Control Panel**.

2. From **Control Panel**, double-click **Network**, click the **Services** tab and then click **Add**.

   The **Select Network Service** dialog box appears.

3. Select **Windows Internet Name Service**, and then click **OK**.

   The **Windows NT Setup** dialog box appears, prompting for the full path of the Windows NT distribution files.

4. Type **C:\I386** and then click **Continue**.

   The appropriate files are copied to your computer, and then the **Network** dialog box appears.

5. Click **Close**.

   A **Network Settings Change** dialog box appears, indicating that the computer needs to be restarted to initialize the new configuration.

6. Click **Yes**.

7. Log on as Administrator.

➤ **To prevent other sources from interfering with WINS**

- If they exist, delete the HOSTS and LMHOSTS files from the %systemroot%\system32\drivers\etc folder.

   This will prevent these files from being used during name resolution in a later section.

Exercise 2
Configuring a DHCP Server for WINS

In this exercise, you will configure the DHCP server to supply the appropriate WINS server addressing information to DHCP clients.

➤ **To start the DHCP Server service**

Note Complete this procedure from the DHCP server only.

1. Click **Start**, point to **Settings**, and click **Control Panel**.
2. Double-click **Services**.

   The **Services** dialog box appears.
3. Click **Microsoft DHCP Server** and then click **Start**.
4. Click **Startup**.

   The **Service** dialog box appears.
5. Click **Automatic** and then click **OK**.
6. Click **Close**.
7. Close **Control Panel**.

➤ **To configure the DHCP server to assign WINS server addresses**

In this procedure, you will configure the DHCP server to automatically assign the WINS server address and NetBIOS node types to DHCP clients.

Note Complete this procedure from the DHCP server only.

1. Click Start, point to Programs, Administrative Tools, and then click DHCP Manager.

   The **DHCP Manager** window appears.
2. Double-click ***Local Machine***.

   The local scope IP address appears.
3. Click the local scope's IP address.

   The local scope options appear under **Option Configuration**.
4. On the **DHCP Options** menu, click **Scope**.

   The **DHCP Options: Scope** dialog box appears.

5. Under **Unused Options**, select **044 WINS/NBNS Servers**, and then click **Add**.

   A **DHCP Manager** message box appears, indicating that for WINS to function properly, you must add the option 046 WINS/NBT node type.

6. Click **OK**.

   The **044 WINS/NBNS Servers** option moves under **Active Options**.

7. Click **Value**.

   The **DHCP Scope: Options** dialog box expands to add the **NBNS Addresses** in priority order values box.

8. Click **Edit Array**.

   The **IP Address Array Editor** dialog box appears.

9. Under **New IP Address**, type your IP address, and then click **Add**.

   The new IP address appears under **IP Addresses**.

10. To return to the **DHCP Options: Scope** dialog box, click **OK**.

11. Under **Unused Options**, select **046 WINS/NBT Node Type** and then click **Add**.

    The **046 WINS/NBT Node Type** option moves under **Active Options**.

12. Under **Byte**, type **0x8** and then click **OK**.

    The **DHCP Manager** window appears with active scope options of **003 Router**, **044 WINS/NBNS Servers**, and **046 WINS/NBT Node Type** listed under **Option Configuration**.

13. Exit **DHCP Manager**.

➤   **To update the DHCP client**

In this procedure, you will renew your DHCP lease, which automatically assigns the new DHCP scope options of WINS server addresses and node type to the client.

Note   Complete this procedure from the DHCP client only.

---

1. Open a command prompt, type **ipconfig /all**, and then press ENTER.

   The **Windows IP Configuration** settings appear. The **Node Type** is listed as **broadcast** and the primary WINS server is not listed.

2. Access the **Microsoft TCP/IP Properties** dialog box.

3. Click **Obtain an IP address from a DHCP Server**.

   A message box asks you to confirm the installation of DHCP.

4. Click **Yes**.

5. Click **OK**.

6. Click **OK**.

7. Switch to a command prompt, type **ipconfig /all** and then press ENTER.

   The **Windows IP Configuration** settings appear. The **Node Type** and **primary WINS server** parameters are updated.

Exercise 3
Using WINS for Name Resolution

In this exercise, you will use the WINS server to perform name resolution from Microsoft Windows NT computers.

➤ **To use WINS for name resolution**

In this procedure, you will use WINS for NetBIOS name resolution. Resolution will be limited to the local subnet, because no remote hosts have registered themselves in the local WINS Server database.

Note Complete this procedure from both computers.

---

1. Open a command prompt and verify that the NetBIOS name cache is empty. Type **nbtstat -c** and then press ENTER.

2. If entries appear, clear the NetBIOS name cache. Type **nbtstat -R** and then press ENTER.

3. Start Windows NT Explorer and attempt to browse other hosts on the local network.

4. Was browsing successful?

   Yes _____

   _____

5. Try to browse \\INSTRUCTOR. Were you successful?

   _No_ _____

   _____

Exercise 4
Installing a WINS Proxy Agent

In this exercise, one computer on each subnet will be configured as a WINS proxy agent to resolve NetBIOS names to IP addresses for non-WINS clients.

➤ **To stop the WINS server**

In this step, you will stop the WINS Server service to prevent it from resolving host names resolution requests.

■ Open a command prompt and type in the following command:

net stop wins

➤ **To use a static IP address**

Note Complete this procedure from the DHCP client only.

1. Access the Microsoft TCP/IP Properties dialog box.
2. Click **Specify an IP address**.
3. Type the following configuration information:

In this box	Type
IP Address	**131.107.**_subnet_id.host_id_
Subnet Mask	**255.255.255.0**
Default Gateway	**131.107.**_subnet_id_**.1**

4. Click **OK**.

The **Network** dialog box appears.

5. Click **OK**.
6. Shut down and restart your computer.

➤ **To test remote NetBIOS name resolution**

In this procedure, you will test name resolution of a remote NetBIOS host without a mapping in the local LMHOSTS or HOSTS files.

Note Complete this procedure from both computers.

---

1. Clear the NetBIOS name cache.
2. Try to browse resources on the \\INSTRUCTOR computer.
3. Was the resolution successful? Why or why not?

    No

➤ **To configure a WINS proxy agent**

In this procedure, you will configure one computer on each subnet to function as a WINS proxy agent. To be a WINS proxy, the client must first be configured as a WINS client.

Note Complete this procedure only from the computers designated by the instructor to be WINS proxy agents. Only one computer on each subnet should complete this procedure.

---

1. Click **Start** and then click **Run**.
2. In the **Open** box, type **regedt32.exe** and then click **OK**.

   The **Registry Editor** window appears.
3. Maximize the **HKEY_LOCAL_MACHINE** window.
4. Open the following registry key:

   SYSTEM\CurrentControlSet\Services\NetBT\Parameter
5. Double-click the **EnableProxy** value.

   The **DWORD Editor** dialog box appears.
6. In the **Data** box, type **1**.
7. Click **OK**.
8. Close the **Registry Editor**.
9. Access the **Microsoft TCP/IP Properties** dialog box.
10. Click the **WINS Address** tab.
11. In the **Primary WINS Server** box, type **131.107.2.200**.

12. Click **OK**.

13. Click **Close**.

    You will be prompted to restart the computer.

14. Click **Yes**.

15. Log on as Administrator.

➤ **To test remote NetBIOS name resolution with a WINS proxy agent**

In this procedure, you will test name resolution of a remote NetBIOS host without a mapping in the local LMHOSTS or HOSTS files, but with a WINS proxy agent configured on each subnet.

Note Complete this procedure from all computers.

1. Try to browse resources on the \\INSTRUCTOR computer.

2. Was the resolution successful? Why or why not?

   No

3. Try to browse resources on a computer on the other student network (but not the proxy agent).

4. Was the resolution successful? Why or why not?

   No

➤ **To remove the WINS proxy agent**

In preparation for the next exercise, you will remove the WINS proxy agent from each subnet.

Note Complete this procedure from the computers designated by the instructor to be the WINS proxy agents. Only one computer on each subnet should complete this procedure.

1. Click **Start** and then click **Run**.

2. In the **Open** box, type **regedt32.exe** and then click **OK**.

   The **Registry Editor** window appears.

3. Maximize the **HKEY_LOCAL_MACHINE** window.

4. Open the following registry key:

SYSTEM\CurrentControlSet\Services\NetBT\Parameter

5. Double-click the **EnableProxy** parameter.

The **DWORD Editor** dialog box appears.

6. In the **Data** box, type **0**.

7. Click **OK**.

8. Close the **Registry Editor**.

9. Access the **Microsoft TCP/IP Properties** dialog box.

10. Click the **WINS Address** tab.

11. In the **Primary WINS Server** box, clear the IP address.

12. Click **OK**.

13. Click **Close**.

You will be prompted to restart the computer.

14. Click **Yes**.

15. Log on as Administrator.

➤   **To start the WINS server**

In this step, you will start the WINS Server service to prepare it for the next lab.

Note   Complete this procedure from the DHCP server computer only.

■   Start a command prompt and type in the following command:

net start wins

Exercise 5 *(optional)*
Overriding WINS

➤ **To update the DHCP client with a static WINS address**

In this procedure, you will override the WINS server address obtained from your DHCP lease and determine what happens as a result.

Note Complete this procedure from the DHCP client only.

---

1. Access the Microsoft TCP/IP Properties dialog box and verify that **Obtain an IP address from a DHCP Server** is selected.
2. Click the **WINS** tab and enter an invalid WINS server address of your choosing.
3. Verify that there is no **LMHOSTS** and no **HOSTS** file (for students who've worked ahead). Also that there is no **DNS** server set up under the **DNS** tab of **Microsoft TCP/IP Properties**.
4. Enter **nbtstat -R** to clear NetBIOS Name Cache. Verify that it is cleared by entering **nbtstat -c**.
5. Reboot the DHCP client.
6. After the machine has reinitialized, click **Start**, and then **Run**, and then enter **\\instructor**.
7. What happens?

   _____

   _____

8. Create an entry in the **LMHOSTS** file

   131.107.2.200   instructor
9. Reboot the DHCP client.

10. After the machine has reinitialized, click **Start**, and then **Run**, and then enter **\\instructor**.

11. What happens?

_____

_____

12. Delete the **LMHOSTS** file just created.

13. Enter **nbtstat -R**.

14. Reattempt step 10. What happens?

_____

15. Remove the manually entered WINS server address and repeat steps 1–6. What happens now?

_____

Lab 13: Maintaining a WINS Database

Objectives

After completing this lab, you will be able to:

■ View the WINS database.

■ Configure WINS replication.

■ Use WINS for name resolution.

■ Configure a static mapping in the WINS database.

Before You Begin

In this lab, you will work with a partner. One of the computers will be a **WINS server** and the other computer will be a **WINS client**.

You will need the following information from your instructor.

When this information is required	Use
Computer name of local host	
Computer name of remote host	

Note Wherever you see the term *%systemroot%*, substitute the name of the directory into which you installed Windows NT.

Estimated time to complete this lab: 60 minutes

Exercise 1
Viewing the WINS Database

In this exercise, you will view the WINS database that is used when resolving computer names to IP addresses.

Note Complete this exercise from the WINS server only.

➤   **To start WINS Manager**

1. Open a command prompt and type **nbtstat -R** to purge the NetBIOS name cache (the -R is case sensitive).

   This verifies that any names in the cache have been removed prior to using WINS for name resolution.

2. Start **Control Panel**, double-click **Services**, and then scroll down the list to verify that WINS has started.

3. What is the name of the service to provide WINS support to clients?

   Windows Internet Name Service

4. Close the **Services** dialog box.

5. Click **Start**, point to **Programs**, **Administrative Tools**, and then click **WINS Manager**.

   The **WINS Manager** window appears.

➤   **To view name to IP address mappings**

In this procedure, you will view the NetBIOS name-to-address mappings that have been registered in the WINS database.

1. On the **Mappings** menu, click **Show Database**.

   The **Show Database** dialog box appears displaying all the NetBIOS names that have been registered in WINS.

2. What NetBIOS names have been registered at the WINS server by the client?

   Student 11, 13

3. How long will it be before the names expire?

   9/1/99

4. Are there any mappings for remote hosts (such as \\INSTRUCTOR)?

   Yes.

5. Click **Close** to return to the **WINS Manager** window.

Exercise 2
Configuring WINS for Replication

In this exercise, you will configure the WINS server to perform database replication with the instructor's WINS server.

Note Complete this exercise from the WINS server computer only.

➤ **To configure the WINS client**

In this procedure, you will configure the WINS client (this is necessary for the WINS server to work correctly).

1. Access the Microsoft TCP/IP Properties dialog box.
2. Click the **WINS Address** tab.
3. Type your IP address in the **Primary WINS Server** box.
4. Click **OK**.
5. Click **Close**.

   You will be prompted to restart the computer.

6. Click **Yes**.

   The computer will restart.

➤ **To configure WINS replication partners**

In this procedure, you will configure the instructor's WINS server as a replication partner.

1. On the Server menu, click Replication Partners.

   The **Replication Partners** dialog box appears showing the local WINS server.

2. Click **Add**.

   The **Add WINS Server** dialog box appears.

3. In the **WINS Server** box, type **131.107.2.200** and then click **OK**.

   The **Replication Partners** dialog box appears with 131.107.2.200 added to the list of WINS servers.

Important The instructor must add your WINS server as a replication partner.

---

4. Under **WINS Server**, click **131.107.2.200**.

5. Under **Replication Options**, click **Configure** next to **Pull Partner**.

   The **Pull Partner Properties** dialog box appears.

   The replication interval is set for 30 minutes.

6. Click **OK**.

➤ **To force replication**

In this procedure, you will force WINS to replicate the WINS database with the instructor's WINS server.

1. From the Replication Partners dialog box, click Replicate Now.

   A **WINS Manager** message box appears indicating the replication request has been queued.

2. Click **OK**.

3. Click **OK** to return to the **WINS Manager** window.

   The **WINS Manager** window appears with 131.107.2.200 added as a WINS server.

4. Under **WINS Servers**, select the local WINS server.

5. On the **Mappings** menu, click **Show Database**.

   The **Show Database** dialog box appears. Under **Select Owner**, notice the addition of all WINS servers that the replication partner (\\INSTRUCTOR) knows about.

Note If the replicated instructor WINS database shows a version ID of 0, repeat steps 1 through 3 again to force replication.

---

6. Under **Select Owner**, select **131.107.2.200**.

   Under **Mappings**, the listing of registered names for the instructor's WINS server appears.

7. View the information in other WINS server databases, and then click **Close** to return to **WINS Manager**.

Exercise 3
Adding a Static Mapping

In this exercise, you will use the WINS server to perform name resolution from both Windows NT computers. A static WINS mapping will be created for a non-WINS client on each subnet so that WINS can resolve its name.

➤ **To use WINS for name resolution**

In this procedure, you will use WINS for NetBIOS name resolution.

Note Complete this procedure from the WINS server computer.

---

1. Start Windows NT Explorer.
2. On the **Tools** menu, click **Map Network Drive**.

   The **Map Network Drive** dialog box appears. This allows you to browse the network.
3. In the **Path** box, type **instructor** and then click **OK**.

   A listing of shared resources appears. You are browsing the **instructor** computer.

➤ **To disable a WINS client**

In this procedure, you will disable WINS support for one WINS client on each subnet. This computer will then be used to demonstrate the benefit of adding a static mapping in WINS.

Note Complete this procedure from only one client computer on each subnet. Use the computer designated as the local host.

---

1. Access the Microsoft TCP/IP Properties dialog box.
2. Click **Specify an IP Address**.
3. Configure the Windows NT client using the following information:

In this box	You type
IP Address	**131.107.**_subnet_id_**.253**
Subnet Mask	**255.255.255.0**
Default Gateway	**131.107.**_subnet_id_**.1**

4. Click the **WINS Address** tab.
5. Remove any entries in the **Primary WINS Server** and **Secondary WINS Server** boxes.

6. Click **OK**.

A dialog box warns you that at least one of the adapter cards has an empty primary WINS address and asks if you want to continue.

7. Click **Yes**.

8. Click **Close**.

A **Network Settings Change** dialog box appears prompting to restart the computer.

9. Click **Yes**.

➤ **To fail WINS name resolution**

In this procedure, you will attempt to resolve a NetBIOS name using WINS. This resolution will fail because the client has not registered its NetBIOS name with WINS.

Note Complete this procedure from all computers except the computer designated as the local host.

---

1. Using **Windows NT Explorer**, attempt to browse the computer designated as the remote host.

2. What was the response?

   Pronceable

   _____

3. Why did the resolution for the remote host fail?

   _____

   _____

➤ **To add a static mapping to the WINS database**

In this procedure, you will add a static mapping into the WINS database to resolve a non-WINS enabled computer. You will then use the static mapping to resolve the non-WINS enabled computer's name.

Note Complete this procedure from the WINS Server computer only. Start with the WINS Manager window active.

---

1. On the Mappings menu, click Static Mappings.

   The **Static Mappings** dialog box appears.

2. Click **Add Mappings**.

   The **Add Static Mappings** dialog box appears.

3. In the **Name** box, type the name of the computer designated as the local host.

4. In the **IP Address** box, type **131.107.***subnet_id***.253** (where *subnet_id* is the local subnet ID), and then click **Add**.

   A blank **Add Static Mappings** dialog box appears.

5. Click **Close**.

   The **Static Mappings** dialog box appears with *local_host* added to the list.

6. To return to the **WINS Manager** window, click **Close**.

➤ **To force replication**

In this procedure, you will force replication of the WINS database in order to ensure that the databases are up to date.

Note Complete this procedure from the WINS Server computer only. Start with WINS Manager active.

1. On the Server menu, click Replication Partners.

   The **Replication Partners** dialog box appears.

2. Click **Replicate Now**.

   A **WINS Manager** message box appears indicating the replication request has been queued.

3. Click **OK**.

4. To return to the **WINS Manager** window, click **OK**.

➤ **To use WINS for name resolution**

In this procedure, you will use the static mapping in WINS for NetBIOS name resolution of the non-WINS enabled computer.

Note Complete this procedure from all computers, except for the computer designated as the remote host.

1. Open **Windows NT Explorer** and browse the resources on the computer designated as the remote host.

   A listing of shared resources appears.

   Success is also indicated by an empty list of shared directories.

2. Close **Windows NT Explorer**.

➤ **To remove a static mapping from the WINS database**

In this procedure, you will remove the static mapping from the WINS database.

Note Complete this procedure from the WINS Server computer only. Start with the WINS Manager window active.

1. On the Mappings menu, click Static Mappings.

   The **Static Mappings** dialog box appears.

2. Select all the entries for the remote host, and then click **Delete Mapping**.

   A **Confirm Deletion** message box appears.

3. Click **Yes to All**.

4. Click **Close**.

➤ **To re-enable the WINS client**

In this procedure, you will re-enable WINS support on the WINS client.

Note Complete this procedure from the computer designated as the local host only.

1. Access the Microsoft TCP/IP Properties dialog box.

2. Click **Obtain an IP Address from a DHCP Server**.

   A **Microsoft TCP/IP** message box appears indicating that DHCP will attempt to automatically configure this computer during initialization.

3. Click **Yes**.

4. Click **Close**.

   A **Network Settings Change** dialog box appears prompting to restart the computer.

5. Click **Yes**.

6. Log on as Administrator.

Exercise 4 *(optional)*
Reversing Roles

- Reverse roles and repeat the lab.

Exercise 5 *(optional)*
Viewing NetBIOS Mappings

➤ **To view the effect of removing a mapping in the WINS database.**

In this procedure, you will view the NetBIOS name-to-address mappings that have been registered in the WINS database and delete the existing mappings to observe the effect.

1. On the Mappings menu, click Show Database.

    The **Show Database** dialog box appears displaying all the NetBIOS names that have been registered in WINS.

2. What NetBIOS names have been registered at the WINS server by the client?

    _____

3. Manually delete the entries for your WINS-enabled client, **STUDENT***x*.

4. From the **STUDENT***x* station, click **Start**, **Run**, and enter **\\instructor**. Were you successful?

    _____

5. Set up another station in the room to register with the WINS server from which the STUDENT*x* registration has been deleted. Reboot this station. From this station, click **Start**, **Run**, and enter **\\Student***x*. Were you successful?

    _____

6. What would you need to do to reregister STUDENT*x* with the WINS server?

    _____

7. What does this mean if the WINS database is deleted?

    _____

Lab 14: IP Internetwork Log on and Browsing

Objectives

After completing this lab, you will be able to:

- Configure a Windows NT Server to use WINS in order to collect domain names for domains that do not span its subnet.
- Plan an LMHOSTS file implementation.

Estimated time to complete this lab: 30 minutes

Exercise 1
Using WINS for Internetwork Browsing

In this exercise, you will use a WINS server to collect the names of remote domains to add to the IP internetwork browse list. **The following exercise is to be done on each computer using Windows NT Server.**

➤ **To configure the WINS Server service for manual starting**

In this procedure, you will disable the WINS Server service so that it will not be used for internetwork browsing or log on validation.

1. Start **Control Panel** and double-click **Services**.

2. Configure the **WINS Server** service for a manual start.

➤ **To disable WINS client support**

In this procedure, you will disable the support for being a WINS client.

1. Access the Microsoft TCP/IP Properties dialog box.

2. Click the **WINS Address** tab and clear all WINS Server IP addresses.

3. Click **OK**.

4. Click **Close** and restart the computer.

5. Browse the network using **Windows NT Explorer**.

6. Which domains do you see? (Refresh the window periodically over the next few minutes as other students are restarting their systems.)

_____

_____

_____

_____

7. Why do you not see the INSTRUCTOR domain (DOMAIN0) and the domains of the other students across the IP router?

_____

_____

_____

_____

➤ **To use WINS to collect the list of remote domains**

In this procedure, you will add WINS support so that a WINS server will be queried for a list of domain names.

1. Access the Microsoft TCP/IP Properties dialog box.

2. Click the **WINS Addresses** tab.

3. In the **Primary WINS Server** box, type **131.107.2.200**.

4. Click **OK**.

5. Click **Close** and restart the computer.

6. Browse the network using **Windows NT Explorer**.

7. Now which domains do you see? (Refresh the window periodically over the next few minutes as other students are restarting their systems)

   Everybody

8. Why do you now see the INSTRUCTOR domain (DOMAIN0) and the domains of the other students across the IP router?

Exercise 2
Planning an LMHOSTS File Implementation

In this exercise, you will decide which computers require an LMHOSTS file to support browsing, logon validation, domain synchronization, and WINS integration, and how each LMHOSTS file must be configured. This exercise is based on the following illustration and scenario.

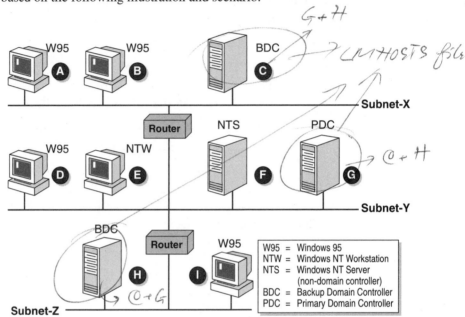

Scenario

As illustrated in the graphic, the domain spans multiple subnets. Each subnet has a domain controller and various other computers. Hosts on each subnet can only browse and access NetBIOS-based hosts on their own subnets because the routers are not configured to forward broadcasts.

1. Which computers require an LMHOSTS file configured to support internetwork browsing? Which computers should be configured in the LMHOSTS file?

1. LMHOSTS Server - LMHOSTS file
2.   "   Client . part of

2. Which computers require an LMHOSTS file to support logon validation? Which computers should be configured in the LMHOSTS file?

None.

A & B -- and G + H
E & F   "   C + H

3. Which computers require an LMHOSTS file configured to support domain account synchronization? Which computers should be configured in the LMHOSTS file?

All domain controllers

C → G + H
H → C + G
G → C + H

4. If a WINS server were installed on Subnet-Y, and all computers were configured to use WINS, which computers would require an LMHOSTS file?

None! B/c all pcs already have IP addr.

Lab 15: Resolving Host Names

Objectives

After completing this lab, you will be able to:

- Configure and use the HOSTS file.
- Configure TCP/IP to use a domain name server (DNS).
- Troubleshoot host name resolution.

Before You Begin

Note Wherever you see the term *%systemroot%*, substitute the name of the directory into which you installed Windows NT.

Estimated time to complete this lab: 20 minutes

Exercise 1
Configuring the HOSTS File

In this exercise, you will add host name/IP address mappings to your HOSTS file, and then use the file to resolve host names.

➤ **To determine the local host name**

In this procedure, you will determine the local host used for TCP/IP utilities, such as PING.

1. Open a command prompt.
2. Clear the NetBIOS name cache.
3. Type **hostname** and then press ENTER.

   The local host name is displayed.

➤ **To ping local host names**

In this procedure, you will ping the name of local host to verify that Microsoft TCP/IP can resolve local host names without entries in the HOSTS file.

1. Type **ping** *hostname* (where *hostname* is the name of your computer) and then press ENTER.

   What was the response?

   pinging successful

2. Type **ping** *hostname* (where *hostname* is the name of another computer on your subnet) and then press ENTER.

   What was the response?

   Successful

➤   **To attempt to ping remote computer name**

1.   Type **ping instructor** and then press ENTER.

2.   What was the response?

     Bad IP addr Instructor

3.   Why were you able to ping local computer names and not remote?

     _____

➤   **To add an entry to the HOSTS file**

1.   Change to the following directory by typing:

     cd   %*systemroot***%\system32\drivers\etc**

2.   You will now use a text editor to modify a file called HOSTS. Type:

     edit HOSTS

3.   Add the following entry to the HOSTS file:

     131.107.2.200   instructorsrv

4.   Save the file, and then exit **Edit**.

➤   **To use HOSTS for name resolution**

1.   Type **ping instructorsrv** and then press ENTER.

2.   What was the response?

     Successful

Exercise 2
Identifying Host Name Resolution Problems

In this exercise, you will copy to your computer a HOSTS file with invalid entries. Then you will run commands that use host names to see how TCP/IP responds when the HOSTS file cannot resolve host names to IP addresses.

➤ **To use HOSTS for name resolution**

1. Rename the HOSTS file in the *%systemroot%*\SYSTEM32\drivers\etc directory to HOSTS.OLD.

2. Copy the appropriate HOSTS file from C:\LabFiles\Lab15 to the *%systemroot%*\SYSTEM32\drivers\etc directory.

If your subnet is	Use this HOSTS file
131.107.3.0	HOSTS.ODD
131.107.4.0	HOSTS.EVN

   Note   You may need to edit the contents of your HOSTS.ODD or HOSTS.EVN file to represent the actual machines in use in your classroom.

3. Rename your HOSTS.ODD or HOST.EVN file to HOSTS.

4. Try to resolve the host name gateway to its IP address. Type **ping gateway** and then press ENTER.

   Four successful "Reply from" messages appear.

5. What kind of TCP/IP host is gateway?

➤ **To test an incorrect IP address**

1. Type **ping router** and then press ENTER.

2. Document the response.

   Request timed out.

3. Use the EDIT command to view the contents of the HOSTS file. Document all entries for the router.

   131. 107. 2. 2   router
   181 107. 2. 1   router

4. Delete the first entry for the router (131.107.2.2).

5. Save and exit the file.

➤ **To test a valid IP address**

1. Type **ping router** and then press ENTER.

2. Document the response.

   Reply from

3. What did you conclude about why the first entry for the router caused errors?

   _Q_

Exercise 3
Identifying Domain Name Server Resolution Problems

In this exercise, you will configure your computer to use a domain name server (DNS), and you will identify problems in the host name resolution process. In this case, the DNS will fail because it doesn't exist.

➤ **To configure DNS support on Windows NT Server**

1. Access the Microsoft TCP/IP Properties dialog box.
2. Click the **DNS** tab.
3. Under **DNS Service Search Order**, click **Add**.

   The **TCP/IP DNS Server** dialog box appears.
4. In the **TCP/IP DNS Server** dialog box, type **131.107.2.200** and then click **Add**.

   The IP address **131.107.2.200** appears in the **DNS Service Search Order** box.
5. Click **OK**.

   The **Network** dialog box appears.
6. Click **OK**.

➤ **To test DNS name resolution problems**

In the following procedure, you will determine the effects of trying to resolve a host name using a DNS, when the DNS is not available.

1. Open a command prompt.
2. Type **ping instructorsrv** and then press ENTER.
3. Document the response.

   Bad IP addr Instructorsrv.

4. Modify the HOSTS file to include the following entry:

   131.107.2.200   instructorsrv
5. Type **ping instructorsrv** and then press ENTER.
6. Document the response.

   Request timed out.

➤   **To remove the DNS configuration**

In the following procedure, you will remove the DNS IP address so TCP/IP will not attempt to use a DNS for name resolution.

1. Access the Microsoft TCP/IP Properties dialog box.

2. Click the **DNS** tab.

3. Under **DNS Service Search Order**, click **Remove**.

   The IP address **131.107.2.200** is removed from the **DNS Service Search Order** box.

4. Click **OK**.

   The **Network** dialog box appears.

5. Click **OK**.

Lab 16: Planning for DNS Server Implementation

Objectives

After completing this lab, you will be able to:

- Estimate the number of DNS name servers needed for a network.
- Estimate the number of DNS domains needed for a network.
- Estimate the number of DNS zones needed for a network.

Before You Begin

This is an instructor-led lab. Your instructor will conduct an open classroom discussion and lead you through the three scenarios in this lab.

The lab consists of three scenario-based exercises. Each exercise describes a company that is migrating to Windows NT Server and wants to implement directory services. You will answer some questions involved in drafting a DNS network design for each company using unique criteria.

The purpose of these exercises is to measure your network planning knowledge prior to installing DNS. This will serve as a baseline to measure how much you have learned at the completion of this course and start you thinking about DNS network design.

Estimated time to complete this lab: 30 minutes

Exercise 1
Designing DNS for a Small Network

The XYZ Company is in the process of replacing their older midrange computer with Windows NT Server 4.0.

Most employees access the midrange system through terminal devices. Some users have 486 computers and a few have Pentium computers; these computers are not networked. The company has already purchased the hardware for the migration.

The network will be used for basic file and print sharing and will also have one Windows NT Server running SQL Server. The majority of users will need access to the SQL Server. Desktop applications will be installed on the local computers, but data files will be saved on the servers.

The XYZ Company would like to be connected to the Internet so they can receive e-mail.

➤ **To draft a network design using the following criteria:**

Environmental components	Detail
Users	100.
Location(s)	Single Office.
Administration	One full-time administrator.
Servers	Three computers, two Pentium 120s with 32 MB RAM, 3.2 GB Hard Disk. One Pentium 150 with 128 MB RAM dedicated to Exchange Server.
Clients	All Pentium and 486 computers, running Windows NT 4.0 or Windows 95.
Microsoft BackOffice applications	Exchange Server and DNS.
Server usage	Basic file and print.

Server application

The design will take into account:

- Number of users
- Number of administrative units
- Number of sites

1. How many DNS domains will you need to configure?

   1 (b/c there's only 01 location)

2. How many subdomains will you need to configure?

   0 (Small company)

3. How many zones will you need to configure?   _'s an area_

   1 (None if selecting ISP)

4. How many primary name servers will you need to configure?

   1 (0 if selecting ISP)

5. How many secondary name servers will you need to configure?

   _1 (0 if   "   o)_

6. How many DNS cache-only servers will you need to configure?

   0 (Small network)

_If we set up subdomains, we need
to set up zones for ea. subdomain._

_DNS1
ZONE
DNS2_

Exercise 2
Designing DNS for a Medium-Size Network

You are consulting for the WXY Company, which has 8,795 users. There are 8,000 users located in four primary sites, with the remaining employees located in 10 branch offices in major U.S. cities. The company has decided to upgrade their existing LANs to Windows NT Servers. The organization has also decided to centralize all user accounts in a single location at the corporate headquarters.

The four primary sites are connected by T1 lines. The branch offices are connected to the nearest primary site by 56 Kbps lines.

Three of the four primary sites are independent business units and operate independently of the others. The fourth is corporate headquarters. Branch offices have between 25 and 250 users needing access to all four of the primary sites but seldom needing access to the other branch offices.

In addition to the 10 branch offices, you have discovered that the company has a temporary research location employing 10 people. The site has one server that connects to Boston via dial-on-demand routers. This site is expected to be shut down within six months. They are a stand-alone operation requiring connectivity for messaging only.

Primary sites will continue to maintain their own equipment and the equipment of the branch offices connected to them. Currently, bandwidth utilization is at 60% during peak times. Future network growth is expected to be minimal for the next 12 to 18 months.

➤   **To draft a network design using the following criteria**

Environmental components	Detail
Users	8,795.
Location(s)	Four primary sites, with 10 branch sites in major cities in the U.S. No plans for opening any international locations.
Administration	Full-time administrators at each of the four primary sites. Some of the smaller sites have part-time administrators.
Number of name servers	To be determined.
Number of cache servers	DNS cache servers will be needed in each of the remote locations for the same zone.
Clients	386, 486, and Pentium computers running Windows NT and Windows 95.
Server applications	SQL Server, Exchange Server and DNS.

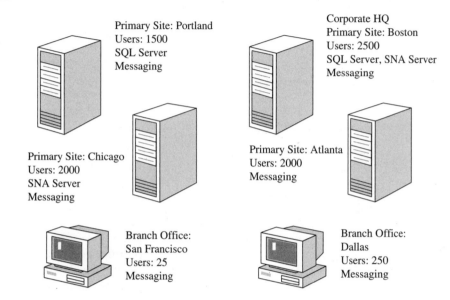

Primary Site: Portland
Users: 1500
SQL Server
Messaging

Corporate HQ
Primary Site: Boston
Users: 2500
SQL Server, SNA Server
Messaging

Primary Site: Chicago
Users: 2000
SNA Server
Messaging

Primary Site: Atlanta
Users: 2000
Messaging

Branch Office:
San Francisco
Users: 25
Messaging

Branch Office:
Dallas
Users: 250
Messaging

Other branch offices include: Los Angeles, 40 users; Salt Lake City, 25 users; Montreal, 30 users; New Orleans, 25 users; Kansas City, 25 users; Washington, D.C., 100 users; Denver, 200 users; Miami, 75 users.

The design will take into account:

- Number of users
- Number of administrative units
- Number of sites
- Speed and quality of links connecting sites
- Available bandwidth on links
- Expected changes to network
- Line of business applications

1. How many DNS domains will you need to configure?

   1 (01 company: XYZ. COM)

2. How many subdomains will you need to configure?

   3 (1 for primary domain + 3 for sub)

3. How many zones will you need to configure?

   4

4. How many primary name servers will you need to configure?

   4 (01 for ea. zone)

5. How many secondary name servers will you need to configure?

   _____

6. How many DNS cache-only servers will you need to configure?

   10 (01 in ea. remote location)

7. Use the following mileage chart to design a zone/branch office configuration based on the geographical proximity between each primary site and branch office. Branch offices should be in the same zone as the nearest primary site.

Portland, OR	Boston	Chicago	Atlanta

Mileage Chart	Atlanta	Boston	Chicago	Portland
Dallas	807	1,817	934	2,110
Denver	1,400	1,987	1,014	1,300
Kansas City	809	1,454	497	1,800
Los Angeles	2,195	3,050	2,093	1,143
Miami	665	1,540	1,358	3,300
Montreal	1,232	322	846	2,695
New Orleans	494	1,534	927	2,508
Salt Lake	1,902	2,403	1,429	800
San Francisco	2,525	3162	2,187	700
Washington, D.C.	632	435	685	2,700

Exercise 3
Designing DNS for a Large Network

The ABC Company has 60,000 users located around the world. The corporate headquarters is in Geneva, Switzerland. North and South American headquarters are located in New York City. The Australia and Asia headquarters are located in Singapore. Each of the regional headquarters will maintain total control of users within their areas.

Users will require access to resources in the other regional headquarters. The three regional headquarters sites are connected by T1 lines.

Each of the three regional headquarters have lines of business applications that need to be available to all sites within their areas, as well as the other regional headquarters. In addition, Malaysia and Australia have major manufacturing sites that all regional subsidiaries will need access to.

These line of business applications are all running on Windows NT Servers. These computers will be configured as servers within the domains.

The links between Singapore, Australia and Malaysia are typically operating at 90% utilization. The Asia and Australia region has 10 subsidiaries comprising Japan, Korea, China, Taiwan, Thailand, Singapore, Malaysia, Indonesia, Australia, and New Zealand.

Due to import restrictions with some of the subsidiaries, it has been decided to give control of the equipment to each subsidiary, and to have a resource domain in each subsidiary. Lately most of the computers the subsidiaries have purchased are running Windows NT Workstation. The company has authorized redundant hardware where you can justify it.

In order to keep this scenario reasonable, the questions and answers deal only with the Australia and Asia region.

➤ **Draft a network design using the following criteria**

Environmental components	Detail
Users in Asia-Australia domain	25,000 evenly distributed across all of the subsidiaries.
Location(s)	Regional headquarters in Singapore, 10 subsidiaries in Australia, China, Indonesia Japan, Korea, Malaysia, New Zealand, Singapore, Taiwan, Thailand.
Administration	Full-time administrators at the regional headquarters and each of the subsidiaries.
Number of domains	To be determined.
Clients	386, 486, and Pentium computers running Windows 95 or Windows NT Workstation.
Server applications	SQL Server, SNA Server, Systems Management Server, Messaging, DNS.
Number of cache servers	To be determined.

The design for the Asia-Australia region will take into account:

- Number of users
- Number of administrative units
- Number of sites
- Speed and quality of links connecting sites
- Available bandwidth on links
- Expected changes to network
- Line of business applications

1. How many DNS domains will you need to configure?

   _____

2. How many subdomains will you need to configure?

   _____

3. How many zones will you need to configure?

   _____

4. How many primary name servers will you need to configure?

   _____

5. How many secondary name servers will you need to configure?

   _____

6. How many DNS cache-only servers will you need to be configure?

   _____

Lab 17: Installing and Configuring the Microsoft DNS Service

Objectives

After completing this lab, you will be able to:

- Install Microsoft DNS Server.
- Configure DNS.

Before You Begin

This lab will use static IP addresses. You will need a partner for this lab. One computer will function as a primary DNS server and the other computer will function as a secondary DNS server.

Estimated time to complete this lab: 30 minutes

Exercise 1
Installing Microsoft DNS Service

In this exercise you will install the Microsoft DNS Server service.

Note Complete this exercise from both computers running Windows NT Server.

➤ **To configure the DNS Service search order**

1. Log on as Administrator.
2. Open a command prompt, type **ipconfig**, and press ENTER.
3. Record the IP address for your computer

   _131. 107. 4. 10_

4. Access the **Microsoft TCP/IP Properties** dialog box and click the **DNS** tab.
5. In the **Domain** box, type your *domain name* from the table:

Computer name	Subnet ID	Domain name	Zone name
STUDENT11	131.107.3.X	ODDA.COM	ODDA.COM
STUDENT13	131.107.3.X	ODDA.COM	ODDA.COM
STUDENT15	131.107.3.X	ODDB.COM	ODDB.COM
STUDENT17	131.107.3.X	ODDB.COM	ODDB.COM
STUDENT19	131.107.3.X	ODDC.COM	ODDC.COM
STUDENT21	131.107.3.X	ODDC.COM	ODDC.COM
STUDENT10	131.107.4.X	EVENA.COM	EVENA.COM
STUDENT12	131.107.4.X	EVENA.COM	EVENA.COM
STUDENT14	131.107.4.X	EVENB.COM	EVENB.COM
STUDENT16	131.107.4.X	EVENB.COM	EVENB.COM
STUDENT18	131.107.4.X	EVENC.COM	EVENC.COM
STUDENT20	131.107.4.X	EVENC.COM	EVENC.COM

Continue this naming scheme to accommodate the actual student configuration.

6. Under **DNS Service Search Order**, click **Add**.
7. In the **TCP/IP DNS Server** dialog box, type in the IP address for your computer, and then click **Add**.
8. Click **OK**.

   The **Network** dialog box appears.

9. Click **OK** to close the **Network** dialog box.

➤   **To install the Domain Name System Server service**

1. Be sure that TCPIP is correctly configured prior to beginning this portion of the lab. If it is not, this lab will be unsuccessful.

2. In **Control Panel**, double-click **Network**, and then click **Services**.

3. Click **Add**.

   The **Select Network Service** dialog box appears.

4. In the **Network Service** list, click **Microsoft DNS Server**, and then click **OK**.

   Windows NT Setup displays a dialog box asking for the full path to the Windows NT distribution files.

5. Type the path **C:\I386** and then click **Continue**.

   All necessary files, including the sample files, are copied to your hard disk.

6. In the **Network** dialog box, click **Close**.

7. When prompted, click **Yes** to restart your computer.

➤   **To install Windows NT 4.0 Service Pack 2**

1. Log on as Administrator.

2. Double-click **C:\Winnt40.sp2\ntsp2.htm** to load the Windows NT Service Pack 2 page.

   The page will load in **Internet Explorer**.

3. Click on the **Install Service Pack** hyperlink.

   This launches SPSETUP.BAT, which will begin the upgrade process.

4. At the **Welcome Screen** click **Next**.

5. In the **Service Pack Setup** dialog box, select **Install the Service Pack**, and then click **Next**.

6. Select **No, I do not want to create an Uninstall directory**, and then click **Next**.

7. Click **Finish** for the Service Pack setup to complete.

   Setup will inspect your computer and then begin to copy the Service Pack files.

   At the end of copying files a dialog box will pop up, notifying you that Windows NT 4.0 has been updated.

8. Click **OK** to restart your computer.

Exercise 2
Viewing the Default Configuration

In this exercise, you will view the default installation of the Windows NT DNS Service.

➤ **To view the default DNS server installation**

Note Complete this procedure from the primary and secondary DNS server computers.

---

1. Log on as Administrator.
2. Click **Start**, point to **Programs**, **Administrative Tools**, and then click **DNS Manager**.
3. On the **DNS** menu, click **New Server**.

   The **Add DNS Server** dialog box appears.
4. In the **Add DNS Server** box, type **Student***x* (where *x* is your student number) and click **OK**.
5. Double-click **Cache**.

   This will display all of the information your DNS server currently has in the cache. All root servers for the Internet are contained in the cache.
6. On the **Options** menu, click **Preferences**.

   The **Preferences** dialog box appears.
7. Click **Show Automatically Created Zones** and click **OK**.
8. Click your computer name and then press F5 to refresh the **Domain Name Service Manager** window.   NS, SoA

   The three reverse lookup zones appear: **0.in-addr.arpa, 127.in-addr.arpa**, and **255.in-addr.arpa**.

9. Click each of the reverse lookup zones. What type of records does each of them contain?

   _____ *all records* NS, SOA _____

10. Double-click **127.in-addr.arpa**.

    A **0** folder appears.

11. Double-click the **0** folder.

    A second **0** folder appears.

12. Double-click the second **0** folder.

    The **PTR** record for **local host** appears. This entry is used when the IP address of **127.0.0.1** is looked up.

    At this point, the DNS service installed on your computer is configured as a caching-only name server.

Exercise 3
Configuring Primary and Secondary DNS Servers

In this exercise you will configure a primary and secondary DNS server.

➤ **To configure a primary DNS server**

Note Complete this procedure from the primary DNS server computer.

1. Right-click your computer name and click **New Zone**.

   The **Creating new zone for Student*x*** dialog box appears.

2. Click **Primary** and then click **Next**.

3. In the **Zone Name** box, type your *zone name* (use the table in exercise 1).

4. Press the TAB key.

   zone name.com.dns is automatically entered in the **Zone File** box.

5. Click **Next** and then click **Finish**.

   The **Server List** now has a zone name and the **Zone Info** entries have been added.

6. Click each of the resource records. What type of records does each of them contain?

   _____

7. Click your zone name (e.g., **odd*x*x.com** or **even*x*x.com**)

8. On the **DNS** menu, click **Properties**.

   The **Zone Properties** dialog box appears.

9. Click the **Notify** tab.

10. In the **Notify List** box, type the IP address of the secondary DNS server for your domain (the IP address of your partner's computer).

11. Click **Add**.

12. Click **OK**.

➤ **To Start Network Monitor**

Note Complete this procedure from the secondary DNS server computer.

1. Start **Network Monitor**.

2. Maximize the **Network Monitor** window and the **Capture Window**.

3. On the **Capture** menu, click **Start Capture**.

➤ **To configure a secondary DNS server**

Note Complete this procedure from the secondary DNS server computer.

1. Right-click your computer name and click **New Zone**.

    The **Creating new zone for Studentx** dialog box appears.

2. Click **Secondary**.

3. In the **Zone Name** box, type your *zone name* (use the table in exercise 1).

4. Type your computer name in the **Server** box.

5. Click **Next**.

    A dialog box displaying **Zone Info** appears. The **Zone Name** box will display your zone name.

6. Press the TAB key.

    zone name.**com.dns** is automatically entered in the **Zone File** box.

7. Click **Next**.

8. In the **IP Master** box, type in the IP address of the primary DNS server (this is the IP address of your partner's computer).

9. Click **Add**.

10. Click **Next** and then click **Finish**.

    The **Server List** now has a zone name, and the **Zone Info** entries that have been added.

Exercise 4
Verify Zone Transfer Using Network Monitor

In this exercise, you will verify that a zone transfer has taken place between the primary and secondary DNS servers.

➤   **To verify the zone transfer**

Note   Complete this procedure from the secondary DNS server computer.

---

1. Switch to Network Monitor.
2. On the **Capture** menu, click **Stop and View**.
3. In the **Summary** window, double-click the frame that has **DNS** listed as the protocol and **OxO:Std Qry Resp**.
4. In the **Detail** window double-click all of the **+DNS** lines.

   The **+DNS** lines expand to show additional detail information.

5. Scroll through the **DNS: Question Section**. What **Question Type** is this?

   Request for zone transfer

6. Scroll down until the first resource record appears. What is the first resource record type?

   Start of zone of authority

7. Scroll down until the second resource record appears. What is the second resource record type?

   Authoritative Name Server

8. Close **Network Monitor**.

Exercise 5
Configuring a Reverse Lookup Zone

In this exercise, you will create a reverse lookup zone that will allow the DNS service to return a name when queried with an IP address from a client.

➤ **To configure a reverse lookup zone for the primary DNS server**

Note Complete this procedure from the primary DNS server computer.

1. Determine the reverse lookup zone name for your primary DNS server by using one of these three methods:

   a. For class A addresses, use your first octet and append to it **.in-addr.arpa**. (Example: A class A IP address of 29.122.15.88 would have a reverse lookup zone name of **29.in-addr.arpa**).

   b. For class B addresses, use your first two octets in reverse order and append to them **.in-addr.arpa**. (Example: A class B IP address of 129.122.15.88 would have a reverse lookup zone name of **122.129.in-addr.arpa**).

   c. For class C addresses, use your first three octets in reverse order and append to them **.in-addr.arpa**. (Example: A class C IP address of 219.122.15.88 would have a reverse lookup zone name of **15.122.219.in-addr.arpa**).

   What is your reverse lookup zone name?

   _____

2. Open the **Domain Name Service Manager** and click on your computer name.

3. On the **DNS** menu, click **New Zone**.

   The **Creating new zone** dialog box appears.

4. Click **Primary** and click **Next**.

5. Type your reverse lookup zone name in the **Zone Name** box.

6. Tab to the **Zone File** box.

   The file name is automatically generated.

7. Click **Next** and then click **Finish**.

8. Double-click the **NS** and **SOA** records and examine the contents.

9. Click your reverse lookup zone name.

10. On the **DNS** menu, click **Properties**.

   The **Zone Properties** dialog box appears.

11. Click the **Notify** tab.

12. In the **Notify List** box, type the IP address of the secondary DNS server for your domain.

13. Click **Add** and then click **OK**.

➤ **To configure a reverse lookup zone for the secondary DNS server**

Note Complete this procedure from the secondary DNS server computer.

1. Determine the reverse lookup zone name for your secondary DNS server.

   What is your reverse lookup zone name?

   107.181. in-addr. arpa

2. Open the **Domain Name Service Manager** and click your computer name.

3. On the **DNS** menu, click **New Zone**.

   The **Creating new zone** dialog box appears.

4. Click **Secondary**.

5. In the **Zone Name** box, type your reverse lookup zone name.

6. Type your computer name in the **Server** box.

7. Click **Next**.

   A dialog box displaying **Zone Info** appears. The **Zone Name** box will display your zone name.

8. Press the TAB key.

   zone name.**com.dns** is automatically entered in the **Zone File** box.

9. Click **Next**.

10. In the **IP Master** box, type in the IP address of the primary DNS server (this is the IP address of your partner's computer).

11. Click **Add**.

12. Click **Next** and then click **Finish**.

Exercise 6
Adding Address and Pointer Resource Records

In this exercise, you will add a host name to your domain.

➤   **To add your other computers as a hosts in your domain**

Note   Complete this exercise from the primary DNS server computer.

---

1. Right-click your zone name.
2. On the menu that appears, click **New Host**.

    The **New Host** dialog box appears.
3. In the **Host Name** box, type your partner's computer name (**Studenty**, where *y* is the student number).
4. In the **Host IP Address** box, type the IP address of **Studenty**.
5. Click **Create Associated PTR Record** and then click **Add Host**.
6. Click **Done**.
7. Click the **107.131.in-addr.arpa** zone and press F5.

    A plus sign (**+**) precedes **107.131.in-addr.arpa**.
8. Double-click **107.131.in-addr.arpa**.

    A folder appears beneath **107.131.in-addr.arpa**.
9. Double-click the folder.

    A **PTR** record appears in the **Zone Info** box.
10. Double-click the **PTR** record, examine the contents of the record, and then click **OK**.

    This is the reverse lookup record that is automatically generated when the **Create Associated PTR Record** option is selected.
11. If necessary, repeat steps 1 through 10 and add a host record for your computer.
12. Verify that there are two **A** records (one record for you, one record for your partner) in your zone.
13. Verify that there are two **PTR** records (one record for you, one record for your partner) in the reverse lookup (107.131.in-addr.arpa) zone.

Lab 18: Installing, Configuring, and Testing a Windows NT FTP Server

Objectives

After completing this lab, you will be able to:

- Install Microsoft Internet Information Server (IIS) FTP services.
- Identify environmental changes made to Microsoft Windows NT 4.0 Server due to the installation of the Microsoft Internet Information Server 2.0 FTP service.
- Use FTP client software to transfer a file.
- Use **netstat** to check the status of the TCP ports.

Estimated time to complete this lab: 15 minutes

Exercise 1
Inspection of Windows NT Server

➤   **To examine the Windows NT Server environment**

1. Log on as Administrator.

2. On the **Start** menu, point to **Settings**, and then click **Control Panel**.

3. In **Control Panel**, double-click **Services**.

    The **Services** dialog box appears.

4. Are any publishing services listed?

    _____

5. Close the **Services** dialog box.

6. Close **Control Panel**.

7. On the **Start** menu, point to **Programs**, point to **Administrative Tools**, and then click **User Manager for Domains**.

    The **User Manager** window appears.

8. Is there an Internet Guest Account listed?

    _____

9. Close **User Manager**.

10. On the **Start** menu, point to **Programs**, point to **Administrative Tools**, and then click **Performance Monitor**.

    Performance Monitor appears.

11. On the **Edit** menu, click **Add to Chart**.

    The **Add to Chart** dialog box appears.

12. Click the arrow next to the **Object** box.

    The list of objects appears.

13. Are there any Internet-related items in the list?

    _____

14. Close the **Add to Chart** dialog box.

15. Close the **Performance Monitor** window.

Exercise 2
Install Internet Information Server

In this exercise, you install Internet Information Server.

➤ **To install Internet Information Server**

1. Log on as Administrator.

2. On the desktop, double-click the **Install Internet Information Server** icon.

   The **Internet Information Server Installation** dialog box appears.

3. In the **Installed from** box, type **C:\I386**.

   The **Microsoft Internet Information Server 2.0 Setup** dialog box appears.

4. Read the information in the **Microsoft Internet Information Server 2.0 Setup** dialog box, and then click **OK**.

5. The following installation options appear:

   • Internet Service Manager

   • World Wide Web Service

   • WWW Service Samples

   • Internet Service Manager (HTML)

   • Gopher Service

   • FTP Service

   • ODBC Drivers and Administration

6. Make sure that only the **Internet Service Manager** and **FTP Service** options are selected, and then click **OK**.

7. When prompted to create the **C:\Winnt\System32\Inetsrv** directory, click **Yes**.

   The **Publishing Directories** dialog box appears, listing the default directory:

   FTP Publishing Directory   **C:\Inetpub\ftproot**

8. Click **OK** to accept the default directory.

9. When prompted to create the default directory, click **Yes**.

   Setup installs the **Internet Information Server FTP Service** software.

10. When Setup is complete, click **OK**.

Exercise 3
Changes Made to the Windows NT Server Environment

➤ **To note the changes made in the Windows NT Server Environment**

1. On the **Start** menu, point to **Settings**, and then click **Control Panel**.

2. In **Control Panel**, double-click **Services**.

   The **Services** dialog box appears.

3. Which publishing services are listed?

   _____

4. Close the **Services** dialog box.

5. Close **Control Panel**.

6. On the **Start** menu, point to **Programs**, point to **Administrative Tools**, and then click **User Manager for Domains**.

   The **User Manager** window appears.

7. Is there an Internet guest account listed?

   _____

8. Close the **User Manager** window.

9. On the **Start** menu, point to **Programs**, point to **Administrative Tools**, and then click **Performance Monitor**.

   Performance Monitor appears.

10. On the **Edit** menu, click **Add to Chart**.

    The **Add to Chart** dialog box appears.

11. Click the arrow next to the **Object** box.

    The list of objects appears.

12. Are there any Internet-related items in the list?

    _____

13. If so, what are the names of the items that can be monitored?

    _____

    _____

14. Close the **Add to Chart** dialog box.

15. Close the **Performance Monitor** window.

Exercise 4
Using FTP to Transfer Files

➤ **To transfer files using FTP**

1. Open a command prompt and type:

   Copy C:\Winnt*.bmp C:\Inetpub\Ftproot

2. Create a temporary directory on your computer called **C:\Ftptemp**.

3. Change to the C:\Ftptemp directory.

4. Start an FTP session with another computer in the classroom by typing the following command:

   FTP Student*x*

   If no other computers are available, start an FTP session with your own server by typing **FTP 127.0.0.1**.

5. Log on as Anonymous.

6. When prompted for a password, press ENTER.

   An **ftp>** prompt will appear.

7. Type the following command at the **ftp>** prompt:

   dir

   A listing of all of the files available at the FTP site appears.

8. Use the **get** command to retrieve a single file. Type:

   get lanma256.bmp

9. To view the transferred file on your computer, type the following:

   !dir

   and then press ENTER.

10. Use the **mget** command to retrieve the rest of the files. Type:

    mget *

11. To exit the FTP session, type:

    Bye

    and then press ENTER.

Exercise 5
Use netstat to Observe TCP Port Activity

➤ **To start an FTP session**

1. Open a command prompt.

2. Start an FTP session with the instructor computer by typing the following command:

   FTP Instructor

3. Log on as Anonymous.

4. When prompted for a password, press ENTER.

   An **ftp>** prompt will appear.

5. Type the following command at the **ftp>** prompt:

   !netstat

   This will display the current TCP network connections.

6. Type the following command at the **ftp>** prompt:

   !netstat -n

   This will display the current TCP network connections and the current TCP port connections.

7. What TCP port does FTP use on the server side?

   _____

   _____

8. To exit the FTP session, type:

   Bye

   and then press ENTER.

Lab 19: Implementing TCP/IP Printing

Objectives

After completing this lab, you will be able to:

- Install a TCP/IP-based printer.
- Connect and print to a TCP/IP-based printer.
- Use LPQ to view TCP/IP print queues.
- Use LPR to print a file.

Before You Begin

You will need the following information.

When this information is required	Use
Printer type	

Estimated time to complete this lab: 30 minutes

Exercise 1
Installing a TCP/IP-based Printer

In this exercise, you will install the Microsoft TCP/IP Printing service, and then use Print Manager to install a TCP/IP-based printer.

➤ **To install the TCP/IP-based printer**

1. In **Control Panel**, double-click **Network**.

   The **Network** dialog box appears.

2. Click the **Services** tab.

   The **Services** property sheet appears.

3. Click **Add**.

   The **Select Network Service** dialog box appears.

4. Click **Microsoft TCP/IP Printing** and then click **OK**.

   The **Windows NT Setup** box appears, prompting you for the full path of the Windows NT distribution files.

5. Type **C:\I386** and then click **Continue**.

   The appropriate files are copied to your workstation, and then the **Network** dialog box appears.

6. Click **Close**.

   A **Network Settings Change** message box appears, indicating that the computer needs to be restarted.

7. Click **Yes**.

8. Log on as Administrator.

9. In **Control Panel**, double-click **Services**.

   The **Services** dialog box appears.

10. Select **TCP/IP Print Server** and then click **Start**.

11. Click **Close**.

➤   **To create a TCP/IP-based printer**

1. In Control Panel, double-click Printers.

   The **Printers** window appears.

2. Double-click **Add Printer**.

   The **Add Printer Wizard** dialog box appears.

3. Click **My Computer** and then click **Next**.

4. Click **Add Port**.

   The **Printer Ports** dialog box appears.

5. Click **LPR Port** and then click **New Port**.

   The **Add LPR compatible printer** dialog box appears.

6. In the **Name or address of server providing lpd** box, type your own IP address.

7. In the **Name of printer or print queue on that server** box, type **tcpprt** and then click **OK**.

8. Click **Close**.

9. Click **Next**.

10. Complete the **Add Printer Wizard** dialog box using the following information:

When prompted for:	Use this information:
Printer manufacturer and model	*Printer type*
Printer name	TCPPRT
Shared / Not shared	Shared
Share name	TCPPRT
Test page	No

    An **Insert Disk** message box prompts you for a floppy disk.

11. Click **OK**.

    A **Windows NT Setup** dialog box appears, prompting you for the location of the Windows NT Server distribution files.

12. Type **C:\I386** and then click **OK**.

    A **TCPPRT** icon appears with the TCP/IP printer created.

Exercise 2
Printing to a TCP/IP-Based Printer

In this exercise, you will connect and print to the TCP/IP-based printer on \\INSTRUCTOR.

➤ **To use Print Manager to connect to a TCP/IP-based printer**

1. In the **Printers** window, double-click **Add Printer**.

   The **Add Printer Wizard** dialog box appears.

2. Click **Network printer server** and then click **Next**.

   The **Connect to Printer** dialog box appears.

3. In the **Printer** box, type the name of the instructor printer: **\\INSTRUCTOR\TCPPRT** and click **OK**.

   The **Add Printer Wizard** prompts you to make this printer the default printer.

4. Click **Yes** and then click **Next**.

5. Click **Finish**.

   An icon representing the shared computer on \\INSTRUCTOR is created in the **Printers** window.

6. Double-click the new printer icon.

   The **tcpprt on INSTRUCTOR** window appears.

7. Start **Notepad**. Then create and print a short document on \\INSTRUCTOR\TCPPRT.

8. Switch back to the **tcpprt on INSTRUCTOR** window.

   A **Messenger Service** dialog box appears, notifying you that your print job has finished printing.

9. Click **OK**.

10. Close the **tcpprt on INSTRUCTOR** window.

➤ **To use LPR and LPQ to access a TCP/IP-based printer**

1. At a command prompt, view the remote print queue. Type:

   lpq -S131.107.2.200 -Ptcpprt -l

   Important   The **-S** and **-P** switches must be in uppercase.

   The **Windows NT 3.5 LPD Server print queue status** appears.

2. Send a new job to the print queue. Type:

   lpr -S131.107.2.200 -Ptcpprt c:\config.sys

   The job is sent to the print queue on \\INSTRUCTOR.

3. View the remote print queue to view new jobs spooled.

   Notice that the new job lists LPR client document as the job name.

4. Exit the command prompt.

Lab 20: Implementing the Microsoft SNMP Service

Objectives

After completing this lab, you will be able to:

- Install the Microsoft SNMP service.
- Use Performance Monitor to view TCP/IP objects.
- Use the SNMPUTIL utility to access SNMP objects.

Estimated time to complete this lab: 30 minutes

Exercise 1
Installing the Windows NT SNMP Service

In this exercise, you will install the SNMP service to view the Performance Monitor objects and counters.

➤ **To view Performance Monitor objects before installing SNMP**

1. Click **Start**, point to **Programs**, **Administrative Tools**, and then click **Performance Monitor**.

   The **Performance Monitor** window appears.

2. On the **Edit** menu, click **Add to Chart**.

   The **Add to Chart** dialog box appears.

3. In the **Object** box, click the arrow to display a list of objects.

4. List the network-related objects. Use the **Explain** button to get an explanation of each counter.

   _____

   _____

   _____

   _____

5. Click **Cancel**.

   The **Performance Monitor** window appears.

6. Exit **Performance Monitor**.

➤ **To install the SNMP service**

In this procedure, you will install the SNMP service to provide counters for monitoring TCP/IP activity.

1. Open **Control Panel** and double-click **Network**.

2. Click the **Services** tab and then click **Add**.

3. Click **SNMP Service**, and then click **OK**.

   A **Windows NT Setup** dialog box appears, prompting you for the full path to the Windows NT distribution files.

4. Type **C:\I386** and click **Continue**.

   The **Microsoft SNMP Properties** dialog box appears.

5. Click **OK**.

   The **Network** dialog box appears.

6. Click **Close**.

   A **Network Settings Change** message box appears, indicating that you must restart the computer.

7. Click **Yes**.

8. Log on as Administrator.

Exercise 2
Monitoring TCP/IP Counters

In this exercise, you will use Performance Monitor to view objects added as a result of installing the SNMP service, and then monitor activity generated by the **ping** command.

➤ **To view the new Performance Monitor objects**

In this procedure, you will view the Performance Monitor objects added as a result of installing the SNMP service.

1. Click Start, point to Programs, Administrative Tools, and then click Performance Monitor.

   The **Performance Monitor** window appears.

2. On the **Edit** menu, click **Add to Chart**.

   The **Add to Chart** dialog box appears.

3. In the **Object** box, click the arrow to display a list of objects.

4. List the TCP/IP-related objects.

   _____

   _____

   _____

   _____

➤ **To monitor IP datagrams with Performance Monitor**

In this procedure, you will use Performance Monitor to view ICMP and IP counter activity generated by the **ping** command.

1. In the **Object** box, click **ICMP** on the list.

   A list of ICMP counters appears.

2. In the **Counter** box, click **Messages/sec**.

3. In the **Scale** box, set the number to **1.0** and then click **Add**.

4. In the **Object** box, click **IP**.

5. In the **Counter** box, click **Datagrams Sent/sec** from the list.

6. In the **Scale** box, set the number to **1.0** and then click **Add**.

7. Click **Done**.

   Your selections appear in the display area.

8. Open the **Options** menu and click **Chart**.

9. Change the **Vertical Maximum** to **10** and then click **OK**.

10. Move the **Performance Monitor** to the top of the screen.

11. Open a command prompt.

12. Ping the instructor's computer.

13. Return to **Performance Monitor**, and view the activity that resulted from the ping.

14. What activity was recorded as a result of using **ping**?

    _____

    _____

15. How many messages per second were recorded for ICMP?

    _1_____

    _____

16. How many IP datagrams were sent per second?

    _1_____

    _____

17. Why were there twice as many ICMP messages as there were IP datagrams sent?

    _____

    _____

18. Close **Performance Monitor**.

Exercise 3
Accessing SNMP Objects

In this exercise, you will view descriptions of MIB objects, and then access SNMP objects to view the data gathered with an SNMP agent and management program.

➤ **To view SNMP data**

In this procedure, you will use the SNMPUTIL.EXE utility to verify that your SNMP agent is configured to communicate with an SNMP manager.

1. Copy C:\LabFiles\Lab20\SNMPUTIL.EXE to C:\WINNT.

2. Open a command prompt.

3. Use **SNMPUTIL.EXE** to determine SNMP objects related to DHCP. Type the following command on one line:

   snmputil getnext 131.107.*subnet_id.host_id*
   public .1.3.6.1.4.1.311.1.3.2.1.1.1

4. How many IP addresses have been leased?

   1   :   131. 107. 4. 0

5. Use **SNMPUTIL.EXE** on the WINS object .1.3.6.1.4.1.311.1.2.1.17. Type:

   snmputil getnext 131.107.*subnet_id.host_id*
   public .1.3.6.1.4.1.311.1.2.1.17

6. How many successful queries have been processed by the WINS server?

   0

7. Use **SNMPUTIL.EXE** on the WINS object **.1.3.6.1.4.1.311.1.2.1.18**. Type:

   snmputil getnext 131.107.*subnet_id.host_id*
   public .1.3.6.1.4.1.311.1.2.1.18

8. How many unsuccessful queries have been processed by the WINS Server?

   0

9. Use **SNMPUTIL.EXE** on the LAN Manager object **.1.3.6.1.4.1.77.1.1.1**. Type:

   snmputil getnext 131.107.*subnet_id.host_id* **public .1.3.6.1.4.1.77.1.1.1** *return 4*

10. Use **SNMPUTIL.EXE** on the LAN Manager Object .1.3.6.1.4.1.77.1.1.2. Type:

    snmputil getnext 131.107.*subnet_id.host_id* **public .1.3.6.1.4.1.77.1.1.2** *return 0*

11. What is the version of Windows NT Server running on the computer? .

    4.0

Lab 21: Troubleshooting an IP Network

Objective

After completing this lab, you will be able to troubleshoot common TCP/IP-related problems in an internetwork.

Before You Begin

Your computer must be running Microsoft Windows NT Workstation or Windows NT Server to complete this lab.

Lab Setup

Make sure the WINS Server service is not started before you begin the exercises in this lab. This should be disabled because the computer will be restarted many times throughout the lab. You must also set your computer to use a static IP address.

Use the following illustration as a reference when troubleshooting problems.

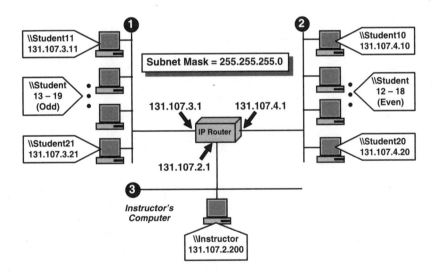

Estimated time to complete this lab: 90 minutes

Exercise 1
Troubleshooting an IP Network

In this exercise, you are given nine scenarios that describe problems common to a TCP/IP installation on a Windows NT-based computer. As you solve each problem, document the symptom or error message, the problem, and the solution.

➤ **To set up your computer for each problem**

1. Open a command prompt.

2. Change to the **C:\LabFiles\Lab21** directory.

3. Run the appropriate batch file:

If your subnet is...	Use this batch file
131.107.3.0	ODD.BAT
131.107.4.0	EVEN.BAT

These batch files will create the **C:\IPTS** directory and copy the appropriate files to it.

4. Change to the **C:\IPTS** directory.

5. Type **ipconfig** and write down the Ethernet adapter name exactly as it appears on the screen:

RTL 80291

6. Using the results from step 5, use the **NICX** batch file to convert the troubleshooting scenarios to you network adapter type. For example, if your results from **ipconfig** were:

Windows NT IP Configuration

Ethernet adapter IEEPRO1

You would type:

NICX IEEPRO1 IEEPRO

If you make a mistake in this step, delete the **C:\IPTS** directory and its contents, and start over from step 1.

7. At the command prompt, type the number that corresponds to the scenario. A batch file will run and implement the problem.

Windows NT will automatically shut down and restart your computer (except in scenarios 2, 5, 8, and 9).

8. Repeat step 7 for each scenario.

Scenario 1

You cannot access any remote hosts using the IP address of the host.

Symptom

Problem

Solution

Scenario 2

You have just installed TCP/IP and cannot ping the following hosts on the network:

- INSTRUCTOR
- GATEWAY

Symptom

Problem

Solution

Scenario 3

TCP/IP does not initialize properly when Windows NT starts.

Symptom

Problem

Solution

Scenario 4

You start Windows NT, and TCP/IP does not initialize properly.

Symptom

Problem

Solution

Scenario 5

When you try to connect to the following computers, you get an error message:

- \\INSTRUCTOR
- \\STUDENT1
- \\STUDENT11

Symptom

Problem

Solution

Scenario 6

You cannot access the server named \\INSTRUCTOR.

Symptom

Problem

Solution

Scenario 7

You are running a batch file that copies files from a server to your workstation. You have noticed that it is taking much longer than normal for the process to complete.

Symptom

Problem

Solution

Scenario 8

You cannot access any remote hosts.

Symptom

Problem

Solution

Scenario 9

You cannot access the computer \\INSTRUCTOR.

Symptom

Problem

Solution

Troubleshooting Hints

Use the following hints to help troubleshoot the problems in Exercise 1.

Resolving Host Names

To resolve host names, use the PING utility in the following order:

1. 127.0.0.1

2. Your own IP address

3. Default gateway IP address

4. Remote host IP address

5. If address resolution is successful, then ping the corresponding host names in the same order as steps 1–4.

6. If host name resolution is not successful, check the HOSTS file for the appropriate entry.

Resolving NetBIOS Names

To resolve NetBIOS names, follow steps 1–4 under "Resolving Host Names," and then:

1. **net view** \\computername

2. If the net view is not successful, verify that the computer is on the local network.

3. If the computer is on a remote network, check the LMHOSTS file for the appropriate entry.

Scenario 1

Normal TCP/IP troubleshooting

Verify TCP/IP parameters

Scenario 2

Normal TCP/IP troubleshooting

Verify HOSTS file

Scenario 3

Normal TCP/IP troubleshooting

Verify TCP/IP parameters

Scenario 4

Check Event Viewer

Verify the TCP/IP bindings

Scenario 5

Normal TCP/IP troubleshooting

Normal NetBIOS troubleshooting

Scenario 6

Normal TCP/IP troubleshooting

Normal NetBIOS troubleshooting

Verify TCP/IP parameters

Scenario 7

Normal TCP/IP troubleshooting

Verify TCP window size

Scenario 8

Normal TCP/IP troubleshooting

Check the ARP cache

Scenario 9

Normal TCP/IP troubleshooting

Check the route table